TREES AND SHRUBS FOR TEMPERATE CLIMATES

TREES AND SHRUBS FOR TEMPERATE CLIMATES

Revised Edition

GORDON COURTRIGHT

Timber
Press

TIMBER PRESS
P. O. Box 1631
Beaverton, Oregon 97075

Courtright, Gordon
    Trees and Shrubs for Western Gardens

© Copyright Timber Press, 1979
1st Printing 1979
Revised Edition 1984

Library of Congress Number 79-65785

ISBN 0-917304-13-6

Printed in the United States of America

Timber Press
P. O. Box 1631
Beaverton, Oregon 97075

CONTENTS

This book is intended to be a visual plant dictionary.

DEDICATION

This book is dedicated to my good wife, Addi, without whose unending help and continual encouragement, this work would never have been completed.

ACKNOWLEDGEMENTS

I wish to express my thanks to the many, many people who helped me along the way. Some for sharing their knowledge about certain plants, some for directing me to good specimens suitable for photography. Special thanks to the following who helped so much when I most needed help.

Mrs. Mai K. Arbegast, Landscape Architect, Berkeley, California.
Mrs. William Bohannon, Horticulturist, Oakland, California.
Dr. Howard C. Brown, Dean of Agriculture and Natural Resources, California. Polytechnic College, San Luis Obispo, California.
Dr. John Bryan, Stribing Arboretum, Golden Gate Park, San Francisco, California.
Mr. Robert Castro, Photography, Oakland, California.
Mr. Joe Class, Photography, Seattle, Washington.
Professor E. Wesley Conner, Department of Horticulture, California Polytechnic College, San Luis Obispo, California.
Mr. Tom Courtright, my son, Nurseryman, Lafayette, California.
Mr. Tochi Domoto, Nurseryman, Hayward, California.
Mr. Glen Handy, Nurseryman, Portland, Oregon.
Mr. Julian Herman, Photography, North Hollywood, California.
Mr. J. Ken Lister, Nurseryman, Gladstone, Oregon.
Mr. Alexander M. McOmie, Nurseryman, Bodega Bay, California.
Mr. Arthur Orans, Photography, Corvallis, Oregon.
Mrs. Muriel Orans, Photography, Corvallis, Oregon.
Dr. Ralph W. Philbrick, Santa Barbara Botanical Garden, Santa Barbara, California.
Mr. Gary Senner, Nurseryman, Woodburn, Oregon.
Mr. Bert Wright, Photography, Aptos, California.

INTRODUCTION

This book is intended to be a practical visual dictionary of all the plants readily obtainable in temperate climate retail nurseries. It is not intended to replace the many excellent botanies written to encompass the many plants sometimes used in gardening. My motive in writing this book grew out of the practical gardening problems I encountered in 40 years of the nursery business trying to assist homeowners with their plant requirements.

The many books written from a botanical point of view have sent gardeners to nurseries looking for plants not commonly propagated and sold. This experience, repeated thousands of times yearly, only leads to frustration for both the misguided and ultimately disappointed gardener and the nurseryman with hundreds of plants in stock, which will serve the gardener's intended purpose equally well. So the first guiding principle of this book is to guide gardeners to the hundreds of fine plants commonly available in the trade which have proved themselves as especially suitable for the growing conditions of temperate zone throughout the world.

Secondly, unlike other gardening books which are usually organized by plant families I have divided the plants into sections by typical height and type, i.e., Low Growing Shrubs, Medium Growing Shrubs, Tall Growing Shrubs, Trees, Vines, and Conifers. I recognize that the height categories will not be entirely valid in many areas throughout the world — first, because plants grow differently in one climatic area than another and further, because many plants are sold (on landscape plans, etc.) to be kept pruned to a given height where they look best.

I have organized the plants by these growth characteristics as a result of my nursery experience. Over the years, I found that most customers came to the nursery looking for a plant to fulfill a specific purpose in a particular place. Frequently, their choice of a specific plant was made from a description in a general horticultural book wherein height and width are seldom mentioned. Hence the second guiding principle of this book is that of growth characteristics so that the reader will not be disappointed by choosing a plant quite unsuitable for its place or purpose.

This principle has been adhered to throughout the book — with the exception of *Azaleas* (all of which will be found in Low Growing Shrubs) and *Rhododendrons* (all of which will be found in Medium Growing Shrubs) and of the Ferns, all listed in the medium section and the Palms which are in the tall section. So, if your planting plans call for a low plant, all the low growing shrubs are to be found in one section in a group together, each accompanied by a color picture.

Thirdly, I have used the language of a nursery catalog, not a botanical book. All too frequently I have found that the scientific nomenclature of the botanist has escaped the lay reader interested only in the beauty of his garden. The language I have chosen will, I hope, assist the reader's comprehension of the plant material available to him.

The plants in each section are listed alphabetically by their botanical names with the common names added. I have followed the names used by the leading, large wholesale nurseries in the United States. I have included the newer names being introduced by the nomenclature committee on plant names. If you know only the common name of a plant look in the *Common to Botanic Name Index* on pages 225 to 231 to guide you to the plant you are seeking.

I have provided two numeric planting indexes for each plant. The first is a temperature guide (shown as temperature zone below which a plant cannot withstand the cold). The second is a planting guide number which indicates the broad cultural requirements of the plant - exposure to sun, drainage and soil requirements.

Thus Zone 9 means the plant's freezing resistance is somewhere between 30 degrees and 20 degrees Fahrenheit depending on how well the plant has hardened off in the fall. But remember that many will freeze at 27 or 28 degrees so the zone guide is merely a clue to put you on your guard.

The same care must be exercised in using the planting guide number. A specific plant may depart slightly in its cultural requirements from those indicated - so use common sense in planting it in a specific location.

Detailed explanations of the meaning of the Zone and Planting Guides will be found immediately following this Introduction and in other places in the book.

In choosing the specimens to illustrate each plant it has been my aim to pick subjects in the five to fifteen year old size. I have endeavored to locate plants which stood alone when possible. In some cases, however, particularly in the case of large bushy plants, vines and hedge plants, I have used a closeup to portray only the foliage in about a one square foot area.

I chose to photograph plants in garden settings rather than using nursery plants in a studio setting, not only to give the reader an accurate impression of what might be expected of the plants in his garden, but also to present landscaping ideas which might prove useful.

The selection of plants included is based entirely on the catalogues of seven of the largest wholesale nurseries in California and Oregon. Some plants listed

in these catalogues were excluded because they are closely related to or indistinguishable variations of plants.

Following the plant listings you will find a number of Indexes to provide you with specific information or particular characteristics. Included are:

Planting Guide

Temperature Guide

Botanical name to Common name with plate number and
    pronunciation dictionary.

Index of Revised Nomenclature Names.

Common name to Botanical name.

White flowering plants.

Yellow and orange flowering plants.

Blue and violet flowering plants.

Red or pink flowering plants.

Plants suitable for seashore.

Fragrant trees and shrubs.

Plants for dry places.

Plants for damp places.

A deer resistant plant list.

An oak root fungus list.

It is my sincere hope that you, the reader, find this work a useful and practical guide to the solution of your gardening problems. If you do, I will feel completely rewarded for the full time job I have had since I retired from the nursery business.

CROSS INDEX OF NEW REVISED NOMENCLATURE NAMES

ALOYSIA TRIPHYLLA	*Lippia citriodora*
ANEMOPAEGMA CHAMBERLAYNII	*Bignonia chamberlaynii*
ARCHONTOPHOENIX CUNNINGHAMIANA	*Seaforthia elegans*
Bignonia capensis	**TECOMARIA CAPENSIS**
Bignonia chamberlaynii	**ANEMOPAEGMA CHAMBERLAYNII**
Bignonia cherere	**DISTICTIS BUCCINATORIA**
Bignonia tweediana	**MACFADYENA UNGUIS-CATI**
Bignonia venusta	**PYROSTEGIA VENUSTA**
Bignonia violacea	**CLYTOSTOMA CALLISTEGIOIDES**
BRACHYCHITON POPULNEUS	*Sterculia diversifolius*
BRAHEA ARMATA	*Erythea edulis*
BRAHEA EDULIS	*Erythea armata*
CAESALPINIA GILLIESII	*Poinciana gilliesii*
CALOCEDRUS DECURRENS	*Libocedrus decurrens*
CHAENOMELES JAPONICA	*Cydonia japonica*
CLYTOSTOMA CALLISTEGIOIDES	*Bignonia violacea*
COLENOEMA PULCHRUM	*Diosma pulchra*
Cydonia japonica	**CHAENOMELES JAPONICA**
CYTISUS x SPACHIANUS	*Genista racemosa*
DIETES IRIDIOIDES	*Moraea iridioides*
Diosma pulchra	**COLEONEMA PULCHRUM**
DISTICTIS BUCCINATORIA	*Bignonia cherere*
ENSETE VENTRICOSUM	*Musa ensete*
Erythea armata	**BRAHEA ARMATA**
Erythea edulis	*Brahea edulis*
Eugenia myrtifolia	*Syzygium paniculatum*
Fremontia	*Fremontodendron*
FREMONTODENDRON	*Fremontia*
Genista racemosa	**CYTISUS x SPACHIANUS**
Gunnera chilensis	**GUNNERA TINCTORIA**
GUNNERA TINCTORIA	*Gunnera chilensis*
HETEROMELES ARBUTIFOLIA	*Photinia arbutifolia*
HIBBERTIA SCANDENS	*Hibbertia volubilis*
Hibbertia volubilis	**HIBBERTIA SCANDENS**
JASMINUM MESNYI	*Jasminum primulinum*
Jasminum primulinum	**JASMINUM MESNYI**
LANTANA MONTEVIDENSIS	*Lantana sellowiana*
Lantana sellowiana	**LANTANA MONTEVIDENSIS**
LEUCOTHOE AXILLARIS	*Leucothoe catesbaei*
Leucothoe catesbaei	**LEUCOTHOE AXILLARIS**
Libocedrus decurrens	**CALOCEDRUS DECURRENS**
Lippia citriodora	**ALOYSIA TRIPHYLLA**
MACFADYENA UNGUIS-CATI	*Bignonia tweediana*
METROSIDEROUS EXCELSUS	*Metrosiderous tomentosus*
Metrosiderous tomentosus	**METROSIDEROUS EXCELSUS**
MICHELIA FIGO	*Michelia fuscata*
Michelia fuscata	**MICHELIA FIGO**
Moraea iridioides	**DIETES IRIDIOIDES**
Murraya exotica	**MURRAYA PANICULATA**

MURRAYA PANICULATA
Musa ensete
Myrtus ugni
OSMANTHUS HETEROPHYLLUS
Osmanthus ilicifolius
PASSIFLORA ALTOCAERULEA
Passiflora pfordtii
Photinia arbutifolia
PICEA ABIES
Picea excelsa
PLATYCLADUS ORIENTALIS
Pleroma grandiflora
Plumbago capensis
Poinciana gilliesii
PSEUDOTSUGA MENZIESII
Pseudotsuga taxifolia
PYROSTEGIA VENUSTA
Rhynochospernum jasminoides
Seaforthia elegans
SENECIO COMPACTUS
Senecio greyii
Sterculia diversifolius
SYZYGIUM PANICULATUM
Tecoma capensis
TECOMARIA CAPENSIS
Thuja orientalis
TIBOUCHINA URVILLEANA
TRACHELOSPERNUM JASMINOIDES
UGNI MOLINAE

Murraya exotica
ENSETE VENTRICOSUM
UGNI MOLINAE
Osmanthus ilicifolius
OSMANTHUS HETEROPHYLLUS
Passiflora pfordtii
PASSIFLORA ALTOCAERULEA
HETEROMELES ARBUTIFOLIA
Picea excelsa
PICEA ABIES
Thuja orientalis
TIBOUCHINA· URVILLEANA
PLUMBAGO AURICULATA
CAESALPINIA GILLIESII
Pseudotsuga taxifolia
PSEUDOTSUGA MENZIESII
Bignonia venusta
TRACHELOSPERNUM JASMINOIDES
ARCHONTOPHOENIX CUNNINGHAMIANA
Senecio greyii
SENECIO COMPACTUS
BRACHYCHITON POPULNEUS
Eugenia myrtifolia
TECOMARIA CAPENSIS
Tecoma capensis
PLATYCLADUS ORIENTALIS
Pleroma grandiflora
Rhynchospernum jasminoides
Myrtus ugni

PLANTING GUIDE

Following each description is a planting group guide. Here again, individual conditions will vary so the planting instructions are general. An attempt has been made to give you a clue to the general soil conditions needed for each plant. You should check local conditions with your nurseryman.

Group 1 means the plant will grow in the sun without special treatment, unless otherwise mentioned.

Group 2 means the plant will grow in the sun, but must have excellent drainage.

Group 3 means the plant will grow in the sun, but must have excellent drainage and only minimum amounts of water, usually gray foliage plants.

Group 4 means the plant will grow in the shade, without special treatment.

Group 5 means the plant will grow in the shade, but must have excellent drainage and special soil mixture.

TEMPERATURE RATINGS

Zone 10	40° to 30° F
Zone 9	30° to 20° F
Zone 8	20° to 10° F
Zone 7	10° to 0° F
Zone 6	0° to –10° F
Zone 5	–10° to –20° F
Zone 4	–20° to –30° F
Zone 3	–30° to –40° F

Temperatures suggested in this book are approximate. The growing conditions, for example, a warm late fall often will keep the plants from hardening off and a sudden early cold snap has been known to freeze plants 20° above the normal freezing point.

BOTANICAL INDEX
and Plate Number
Pronunciation and the Common Names

BOTANICAL NAME	PRONUNCIATION	COMMON NAME (or newer botanical name)	PLATE NUMBER
Abelia 'Edward Goucher'	A-beel-i-a	Pink Abelia	111
Abelia grandiflora		Glossy Abelia	112
Abies balsamea nana	Ay-bees	Dwarf Balsam Fir	569
Abies concolor		White Fir	570
Abies lasiocarpa		Alpine Fir	571
Abies pinsapo 'Glauca'		Blue Spanish Fir	572
Abutilon	A-beau-ti-lon	Flowering Maple	113
Acacia baileyana	A-kay-shi-a	Bailey Acacia	369
Acacia baileyana 'Purpurea'		Purple Leaf Baileyana	370
Acacia longifolia		Golden Wattle	371
		(*A. latifolia*)	
Acacia melanoxylon		Blackwood Acacia	372
Acacia verticillata		Star Acacia	373
Acanthus mollis	A-kanth-us	Bear's Breech	1
Acer circinatum	Ay-ser	Vine Maple	374
Acer dasycarpum		Acer Saccharinum	382
Acer japonica 'Acontifolium		Fern Leaf Full Moon Maple	375
Acer palmatum		Japanese Maple	376
Acer palmatum 'Atropurpureum'		Red Japanese Maple	377
Acer palmatum 'Dissectum'		Red Cutleaf Maple	2
Acer palmatum 'Dissectum Everred'		Red Cutleaf Maple	3
Acer palmatum 'Dissectum Viridis'		Green Cutleaf Maple	4
Acer palmatum 'Sangokaku'		Japanese Coral Bark Maple	378
Acer platanoides		Norway Maple	379
Acer platanoides 'Schwedleri'		Schwedleri Maple	380
Acer platanoides 'Crimson King'		Crimson King Maple	381
Acer saccharinum		Silver Maple	382
		(*A. dasycarpum*)	
Adiantum pedatum	Ad-i-an-tum	Five Finger Fern	168
Aesculus carnea 'Briotii'	Es-keu-lus	Red Horsechestnut	383
Aesculus hippocastanum		White Horsechestnut	384
Agapanthus africanus	Ag-a-pan-thus	Lily Of The Nile	5
Agapanthus africanus 'Peter Pan'		Dwarf Lily Of The Nile	6
Agave attenuata	Ah-gah-ve	Agave	7
Albizia julibrissin	Al-biz-i-a	Silktree, Pink Acacia Or Mimosa	385
Alnus cordata	All-nus	Italian Alder	386
Alnus rhombifolia		White Alder	387
Alsophila australis	Al-sof-il-a	Australian Tree Fern	169

BOTANICAL NAME	PRONUNCIATION	COMMON NAME (or newer botanical name)	PLATE NUMBER
Althaea chinensis syriacus	Al-thee-a	Rose Of Sharon	114
Ampelopsis	Am-pe-lop-sis	Parthenocissus	522
Ampelopsis quinquefolia		Virginia Creeper	522
Ampelopsis tricuspidata		Boston Ivy	523
Andromeda polifolia	An-drom-e-da	Bog Rosemary	8
Aralia papyrifera	A-ray-lia	Rice Paper Plant	261
Aralia elegantissima		False Aralia	115
		(Dizygotheca elegantissima)	
Aralia sieboldii		Glossy Aralia	116
		Fatsia japonica	
Araucaria araucana	Ahr-a-kair-ia	Monkey Tree	573
		(A. imbricata)	
Araucaria bidwillii		Bunya-Bunya	574
Araucaria excelsa		Star Pine, Norfolk Island Pine	575
Arctostaphylos densiflora 'Howard McMinn'	Ark-to-staf-il-os	Howard McMinn Manzanita	9
Arctostaphylos hookeri		Monterey Manzanita	10
Arctostaphylos uva ursi		Kinnikinnick Or Bear Berry	11
Arbutus menziesii	Ar-bu-tus	Madrone	388
Arbutus unedo		Strawberry Tree	262
Arbutus unedo 'Compacta'		Dwarf Strawberry Tree	117
Asparagus meyeri	As-par-a-gus	Meyeri	169
Asparagus sprengeri		Sprengeri	170
Aspidium capense	As-pid-i-um	Leather Leaf Fern	171
Aspidistra elatior	As-pi-dis-tra	Cast Iron Plant	12
Asplenium bulbiferum	As-plee-ni-um	Mother Fern	172
Aucuba japonica	Au-keu-ba	Dwarf Aucuba	118
Aucuba japonica 'Crotonifolia'		Croton Leaf Aucuba	119
Aucuba japonica 'Picturata'		Gold Leaf Aucuba	120
Aucuba japonica 'Variegata'		Gold Dust Aucuba	121
Azara microphylla	A-za-ra	Box Leaf Azara	263
Azalea evergreen	A-zay-le-a	Azalea (*Rhododendron*)	13
Azalea deciduous		Azalea (*Rhododendron*)	13
Bambusa phyllostachys aurea	Bam-bu-sa	Golden Bamboo	264
Bambusa phyllostachys bambusoides		Giant Timber Bamboo	265
Bambusa phyllostachys nigra		Black Bamboo	266
Bambusa sasa pygmaea		Sasa Bamboo	14
Bauhinia purpurea	Ba-hin-i-a	Orchid Tree	389
Beaucarnea recurvata	Bo-car-ne-a	Pony Tail	267
Beaumontia grandiflora	Bo-mon-ti-a	Easter Lily Vine	524
Beloperone guttata	Bel-o-per-o-ne	Shrimp Plant	15
Berberis darwinii	Ber-ber-is	Darwin Barberry	122
Berberis julianae		Wintergreen Barberry	123
Berberis thunbergii 'Atropurpurea'		Japanese Barberry	124
Betula alba	Bet-u-la	White Birch	390
Betula alba papyrifera		Cutleaf White Birch	392
Betula alba 'Laciniata'		Canoe Or Paper Birch	391
Betula alba 'Youngii'		Young's Birch	393

BOTANICAL NAME	PRONUNCIATION	COMMON NAME (or newer botanical name)	PLATE NUMBER
Bignonia cherere	Big-non-ia	Scarlet Trumpet Vine (*Phaedranthus*)	525
Bignonia venusta		Flame Vine (Pyrostegia)	526
Bignonia violacea		Lavender Trumpet Vine (*Clytostoma*)	527
Bougainvillea in variety	Bou-gayn-vil-le-a	Bougainvillea	528 to 534
Bouvardia 'Albatross'	Bo-var-di-a	Bouvardia	16
Brunfelsia calycina floribunda	Brun-fel-si-a	Yeaterday, Today And Tomorrow Shrub	125
Buxus japonica	Buk-sus	Japanese Boxwood	17
Buxus sempervirens		English Boxwood	126
Buxus sempervirens 'Suffruticosa'		Dwarf English Boxwood	18
Calliandra inequilatera	Kal-i-an-dra	Pink Powder Puff	127
Calliandra tweedii		Brazilian Flame Bush	128
Callistemon lanceolatus	Kal-li-ste-mom	Bottlebrush	268/394
Callistemon viminalis		Weeping Bottlebrush	269/395
Calluna vulgaris 'H.E. Beale'	Ka-lu-na	Scotch Heather	19
Calluna vulgaris 'Searlei'		Scotch Heather	20
Camellias	Ka-mel-i-a	Camellias	129/130
Camphora officinarum	Kamp-for	Camphor Tree Cinnamomum Camphor	396
Campsis tagliabuana	Kamp-sis	Trumpet Creeper	535
Carissa grandiflora	Ka-ris-a	Natal Plum	131
Carissa grandiflora 'Prostrata'		Dwarf Natal Plum	21
Carpenteria californica	Kar-pen-te-ri-a	Bush Anemone	270
Carpinus betulus 'Columnaris'	Kar-pin-us	European Hornbean	397
Cassia artemisioides	Kas-si-a	Wormwood Senna	132
Catalpa speciosa	Ka-tal-pa	Western Catalpa	398
Ceanothus arboreus 'Ray Hartman'	See-a-no-thus	Ray Hartman Ceanothus	271
Ceanothus cyaneus, 'Sierra Blue'		Sierra Blue Ceanothus	272
Ceanothus glorious		Point Reys Creeper	22
Ceanothus griseus horizontalis		Carmel Creeper	23
Ceanothus impressus		Santa Barbara Ceanothus	133
Ceanothus 'Julia Phelps'		Ceanothus Julia Phelps	134
Ceanothus 'Mountain Haze'		Ceanothus Mountain·Haze	135
Cedrus atlantica	Se-drus	Atlas Cedar	576
Cedrus atlantica 'Glauca'		Blue Cedar	577
Cedrus atlantica 'Glauca pendula'		Weeping Blue Cedar	578
Cedrus deodara		California Christmas Tree	579
Cedrus deodara 'Aurea'		Golden Deodar	580
Cedrus deodara 'Prostrata'		Weeping Deodar	581
Cedrus libani		Cedar Of Lebanon	582
Ceratonia siliqua	Ser-a-tone-i-a	Carob Or St. John's Bread	399
Ceratostigma plumbaginoides	Ser-a-to-stig-ma	Blue Leadwort	24
Cercis canadensis	Ser-sis	Eastern Redbud	273
Cercis occidentalis		Western Redbud	274
Cestrum parqui	Ses-trum	Nightblooming Jessamine	136

BOTANICAL NAME	PRONUNCIATION	COMMON NAME (or newer botanical name)	PLATE NUMBER
Chamaecyparis lawsoniana	Kam-e-sip-a-ris	Port Orford Cedar	583
Chamaecyparis lawsoniana 'Allumii'		Blue Lawson	584
Chamaecyparis lawsoniana 'Ellwoodii'		Ellwood Cypress	585
Chamaecyparis lawsoniana 'Nidiformis'		Bird Nest Cypress	586
Chamaecyparis obtusa		Hinoki Cypress	587
Chamaecyparis obtusa 'Aurea'		Golden Hinoki Cypress	588
Chamaecyparis obtusa 'Crippsii'		Crippsi Cypress	589
Chamaecyparis obtusa 'Minima'			590
Chamaecyparis obtusa 'Nana'		Dwarf Hinoki Cypress	591
Chamaecyparis obtusa 'Torulosa'		Twisted Hinoki Cypress	592
Chamaecyparis pisifera 'Cyano Viridis'		Blue Plume Cypress	593
Chamaecyparis pisifera 'Filifera'		Threadbranch Cypress	594
Chamaecyparis pisifera 'Filifera Aurea'		Golden Threadbranch Cypress	594
Chamaecyparis pisifera 'Plumosa'		Plume Cypress	595
Chamaelaucium ciliatum	Kam-ae-lau-si-um	Geraldton Wax Flower (*C. uncinatum*)	137
Chamaerops excelsa	Ka-me-rops	Windmill Palm *Trachycarpus fortunnei*	317
Chamaerops humilis		Mediterranean Fan Palm	318
Choisya ternata	Choice-c-a	Mexican Orange	138
Chorisia speciosa	Ko-ris-e-a	Floss Silk Tree	400
Cinnamomum camphora	Sin-a-mo-mum	Camphor Tree (*Camphora officinarum*)	396
Cissus antarctica	Sis-us	Kangaroo Ivy	536
Cissus capensis		Evergreen Grape (*Rhoicissus*)	537
Cissus rhombifolia		Grape Ivy (*Vitis rhombifolia*)	538
Cistus corbariensis	Sis-tus	White Rock Rose	25
Cistus ladaniferus Maculatus		Crimson Spot Rock Rose	26
Cistus purpureus		Orchid Rock Rose	27
Citrus	Sit-rus	Citrus	139 to 142
Clematis armandii	Klem-a-tis	Evergreen Clematis	539
Clematis, deciduous in variety		Clematis	540
Clivia miniata	Kli-vi-a	Kafir Lily	28
Clytostoma	Kly-tos-tom-ah	Bignonia	527
Cocculus laurifolius	Kok-u-lus	Laurelleaf Snail Seed	275
Cocos australis	Ko-kus	Hardy Blue Cocos (*Butia capitata*)	319
Cocos plumosa		Queen Palm (*Arecastrum romanzoffianum*)	320
Coleonema	Ko-le-nee-mah	Diosma	42
Convolvulus cneorum	Kon-vol-veu-lus	Bush Morning Glory	29
Coprosma baueri	Ko-pros-ma	Mirror Plant	143
Coprosma baueri 'Aurea'		Golden Mirror Plant	30
Coprosma kirkii		Creeping Mirror Plant	31
Cordyline indivisa	Kor-di-li-ne	Dracaena Palm (*D. indivisa*)	285
Cordyline stricta		Palm Lily	144

BOTANICAL NAME	PRONUNCIATION	COMMON NAME (or newer botanical name)	PLATE NUMBER
Cornus	Kor-nus	Dogwood	401
Cornus florida		Eastern Dogwood	401
Cornus florida rubra		Pink Dogwood	402
Cornus florida 'Welchii'		Variegated Dogwood	403
Cornus nuttallii		Western Dogwood	404
Cornus nuttalii 'Goldspot'		Variegated Western Dogwood	405
Corokia cotoneaster	Cor-ok-e-a	Cotoneaster Corokia	145
Correa pulchella	Kor-re-a	Australian Fuchsia	32
Cortaderia selloana	Kor-ta-der-i-a	Pampas Grass (C. argentea)	276
Corylus avellana contorta	Kor-i-lus	Twisted Filbert Or Walking Stick	146
Cotinus coggygria	Ko-ti-nus	Smoke Tree (Rhus cotinus)	277
Cotoneaster dammeri	Ko-to-ne-as-ter	Bearberry Cotoneaster	33
Cotoneaster franchetii		Franchet Cotoneaster	279
Cotoneaster glaucophylla		Bright Bead Cotoneaster	34
Cotoneaster horizontalis		Rock Cotoneaster	35
Cotoneaster microphylla		Rockspray Cotoneaster	36
Cotoneaster pannosa		Silver-leaf Cotoneaster	280
Cotoneaster parneyi		Red Cluster Cotoneaster	281
Crassula argentea	Kras-u-la	Jade Plant	147
Crataegus	Kra-te-gus	Hawthorn	406
Crataegus contorta		Snake Hawthorne	148
Crataegus cordata		Washington Thorn	406
Crataegus lavallei		Crataegus Carrieri	407
Crataegus oxyacantha 'Paulii'		Paul Scarlet Hawthorn	408
Crotalaria agatiflora	Krot-a-la-ri-a	Canary Bird Bush	149
Cryptomeria japonica 'Elegans'	Krip-to-me-ri-a	Japanese Cedar	596
Cryptomeria japonica 'Elegans Nana'		Compact Japanese Cedar	597
Cupaniopsis anacardioides	Cup-ain-e-op-is	Carrot Wood	409
Cupressocyparis leylandii	Kew-press-o-sip-a-ris	Leyland Cypress	598
Cupressus glabra	Ku-press-us	Arizona Cypress	599
Cupressus macrocarpa		Monterey Cypress	600
Cupressus semperivrens 'Glauca'		Italian Cypress	601
Cycas revoluta	Sy-kas	Sago Palm	321
Cydonia japonica	Sy-doh-ni-a	Flowering Quince (chaenomeles)	150
Cyperus alternifolius	Sy-per-os	Umbrella Flatsedge	37
Cyperus papyrus		Egyptian Paper Reed	282
Cyrtomium falcatum	Ser-to-mi-um	Holly Fern	173
Cytisus in variety	Si-tis-us	Scotch Broom	151 to 155
Daphne cneorum	Daf-ne	Rock Daphne	38
Daphne odora		Winter Daphne	39
Daphne burkwoodii 'Somerset'			40
Datura suaveolens	Day-tu-ra	Angel's Trumpet	283
Daubentonia tripetii	Daub-en-ton-ia	Scarlet Wisteria Tree	156
Deutzia gracilis	Dut-zi-a	Deutzia	41
Dicksonia antarctica	Dick-so-ne-a	New Zealand Or Tasmanian Tree Fern	174

BOTANICAL NAME	PRONUNCIATION	COMMON NAME (or newer botanical name)	PLATE NUMBER
Diosma pulchrum	Di-oz-ma	Pink Breath Of Heaven *(Coleonena)*	42
Diosma reevesi		Baby's Breath *(Coleonena)*	43
Diospyros kaki	Dy-os-po-ros	Persimmon	410
Dodonaea viscosa purpurea	Do-don-ea	Hopseed Bush	284/411
Dracaena indivisa	Dra-se-na	Cordyline Indivisa *(Dracaena Palm)*	285
Echium fastuosum	Ek-i-um	Pride Of Madeira	157
Elaeagnus pungens	El-ee-agnus	Silver Berry	286
Elaeagnus pungens 'Maculata'		Gold Edge Elaeagnus	287
Equisetum hyemale	Ek-wi-se-tum	Horsetail Reed Grass	44
Erica melanthera	E-ri-ka	Scotch Heather	158/159
Erica carnea 'Springwood'		Spring Heath	45/46
Eriobotrya deflexa	E-ri-bot-ri-a	Bronze Loquat *(Photinia deflexa)*	412
Euryops			48
Eriobotrya japonica		Loquat	413
Eriogonum arborescens	Er-i-ogon-um	Buckwheat	47
Erythea armata	Er-i-the-a	Mexican Blue Fan Palm	322
Erythea edulis		Guadalupe Fan Palm	323
Escallonia 'Fradesii'	Es-ka-lon-ia	Pink Princess Escallonia	288
Escallonia montevidensis		Montevideo Escallonia	289
Escallonia organensis		Pink Escallonia	290
Escallonia rubra		Red Escallonia	160
Eucalyptus citriodora	U-ka-lip-tus	Lemon Scented Gum	414
Eucalyptus ficifolia		Red Flowering Gum	415/416
Eucalyptus globulus		Blue Gum	417
Eucalyptus globulus 'Compacta'		Dwarf Blue Gum	418
Eucalyptus lehmannii		Bushy Yate	419
Eucalyptus polyanthemos		Red Box Gum	420
Eucalyptus pulverulenta		Dollar Leaf Gum	421
Eucalyptus sideroxylon rosea		Red Iron Bark Gum	422
Eucalyptus viminalis		Ribbon Gum	423
Eugenia myrtifolia	U-jean-e-a	Brush Cherry *(Syzygium paniculatum)*	291
Eugenia myrtifolia 'Compacta'		Dwarf Brush Cherry *(Dwarf syzygium paniculatum)*	161
Euonymus alata	Eu-on-i-mus	Burning Bush	162
Euonymus japonica		Evergreen Euonymus	163
Euonymus japonica 'Aureo-marginata'		Golden Euonymus	164
Euonymus japonica 'Aureo-variegata'		Gold Spot Euonymus	165
Euonymus japonica 'Silver Queen'		Silver Queen Euonymus	166
Euryops pectinatus	Uri-ops	Euryops	48
Fagus sylvatica	Fa-gus	Green Beech	424
Fagus sylvatica 'Atropunicea'		Copper Beech	425
Fagus sylvatica 'Tricolor'		Tricolor Beech	426
Fatshedera lizei	Fat-sa-hed-ra	Botanical Wonder	541
Feijoa sellowiana	Fe-hoy-a	Pineapple Guava	292

BOTANICAL NAME	PRONUNCIATION	COMMON NAME (or newer botanical name)	PLATE NUMBER
Festuca glauca	Fes-tu-ka	Festuca	49
Ferns			
Adiantum pedatum	Ad-i-an-tum	Five Finger Fern	167
Alsophilla australis	Al-sof-il-a	Australian Tree Fern	168
Asparagus meyerii	As-par-a-gus	Meyeri	169
Asparagus sprengerii		Sprengeri	170
Aspidium capense	As-pid-i-um	Leather Leaf Fern	171
Asplenium bulbiferum	As-plee-ni-um	Mother Fern	172
Cyrtomium falcatum	Ser-to-mi-um	Holly Fern	173
Dicksonia antarctica	Dick-so-ne-a	New Zealand Tree Fern	174
Nephrolepis exaltata	Ne-fro-lep-is	Boston Sword Fern	175
Pellaea rotundifolia	Pel-lee-a	Round Leaf Fern	176
Polystichum angulare	Po-lis-ti-kum	Single Mother Fern	177
Polystichum munitum		Western Sword Fern	178
Polystichum setosum		Japanese Lace Fern	179
Platycerium alcicorne	Plat-i-se-ri-um	Staghorn Fern	180
Platycerium grande		Staghorn Fern	181
Woodwardia chamissoi	Wood-war-di-a	Giant Chain Fern *(W. fimbriata)*	182
Ficus benjamina	Fi-kus	Weeping Fig	293/427
Fiscus elastica 'Decora'		Rubber Tree	294/428
Ficus retusa nitida		Indian Laurel	295/429
Ficus repens		Creeping Fig	542
Forsythia	For-sith-i-a	Forsythia	185
Fraxinus uhdei	Frax-in-us	Shamel Ash	430
Fraxinus velutina 'Glabra'		Modesto Ash	431
Fremontia californica	Fre-mon-ti-a	Flannel Bush	296
Fuchsias	Few-Sha	Fuchsia	182 to 184
Gardenia mystery	Gar-de-ni-a	Mystery Cape Jasmine	50
Gardenia radicans		Cape Jasmine	51
Gardenia veitchi		Veitchi Cape Jasmine	52
Garrya elliptica	Gar-ri-a	Silk Tassel Bush	186
Gaultheria procumbens	Gaul-ther-i-a	Dwarf Lemon Leaf	53
Gaultheria shallon		Salal, Lemon Leaf	54
Gelsemium sempervirens	Jel-se-mi-um	Carolina Jessamine	543
Genista racemosa	Jen-is-ta	Sweet Broom	187
Ginkgo biloba	Gink-go	Maidenhair Tree	432
Gleditsia triacanthos inermis	Gle-dit-si-a	Honey Locust	433
Gleditsia triacanthos 'Moraine'		Moraine Locust	434
Gleditsia triacanthos 'Shademaster'		Shademaster Locust	435
Gleditsia triacanthos 'Sunburst'		Sunburst Locust	436
Grevillea robusta	Gre-vil-e-a	Silk Oak	437
Grevillea noellii		Noelli	55
Grewia caffra	Grew-e-a	Lavender Starflower	297
Griselinia littoralis	Gri-se-lin-ia	Kupuka Tree	298
Gunnera chilensis	Gun-er-a	Gunnera	188
Hakea suaveolens	Ha-ke-a	Sweet Hakea	299
Harpephyllum caffrum	Harp-a-phil-e-um	Kafir Plum	438

BOTANICAL NAME	PRONUNCIATION	COMMON NAME (or newer botanical name)	PLATE NUMBER
Hebe buxifolia	He-be	Veronica buxifolia	56
Hebe 'Coed'		Veronica Co-ed	57
Hebe Evansii		Veronica rubra	58
Hebe imperialis		Veronica imperialis	59
Hebe menziesii		Veronica menziesii	60
Hebe 'Patty's Purple'		Veronica Patty's Purple	61
Hedera canariensis	Hed-ra	Algerian Ivy	544
Hedera helix		English Ivy	545
Hedera helix 'Hahnsii'		Hahn's Ivy	546
Helleborus lividus corsicus	Hel-le-bor-us	Corsican Hellebore	62
Hibbertia volubilis	Hi-ber-ti-a	Guinea Gold Vine	547
Hibiscus moscheutos	Hi-bis-kus	Rose Mallow	189
Hibiscus rosa-sinensis		Hibicus	190
Hydrangea paniculata 'Pee Gee'	Hy-dran-je-a	Pee Gee Hydrangea	300
Hydrangea hortensis		Hydrangea	191/192
Hymenosporum flavum	Hi-men-os-por-um	Sweet Shade	439
Hypericum calycinum	Hi-per-e-kum	Aaron's Beard	63
Hypericum moserianum		Gold Flower	64
Hypericum patulum henryi		St. John's Wort	65
Ilex altaclarensis 'Wilsonii'	I-lex	Wilson Holly	301/440
Ilex aquifolium		English Holly	302
Ilex aquifolium 'Variegata'		Variegated English Holly	303
Ilex cornuta 'Burfordii'		Bufford Holly	193
Ilex cornuta 'Rotunda'		Dwarf Japanese Holly	66
Ilex crenata 'Green Island Holly'		Green Island Holly	67
Jacaranda mimosaefolia	Jak-a-ran-da	Jacaranda	441
Jasminum magnificum	Jas-min	Angel Wing Jasmine (J. nitidum)	68/548
Jasminum polyanthum		Pink Jasmine	549
Jasminum primulinum		Primrose Jasmine (J. mesnyi)	550
Juniperus chinensis 'Armstrongii'	Ju-nip-er-us	Armstrong Juniper	602
Juniperus chinensis 'Armstrongii Coasti'		Coasti Juniper	603
Juniperus chinensis 'Blaauwii'		Blaauw's Juniper	604
Juniperus chinensis 'Blue Point'		Blue Point Juniper	605
Juniperus chinensis 'Hetzii Glauca'		Hetzii Glauca Juniper	606
Juniperus chinensis 'Pfitzeriana'		Pfitzer Juniper	607
Juniperus chinensis 'Pfitzeriana Aurea'		Gold Pfitzer	608
Juniperus chinensis 'Pfitzeriana Glauca'		Blue Pfitzer	609
Juniperus chinensis 'Procumbens'		Japanese Garden Juniper	610
Juniperus chinensis 'Procumbens Nana'		Compact Garden Juniper	611
Juniperus chinensis 'Robusta Green'		Robusta Juniper	612
Juniperus chinensis 'San Jose'		San Jose Juniper	613
Juniperus chinensis 'Sea Green'		Sea Green Juniper	614
Juniperus chinensis 'Torulosa'		Hollywood Juniper	615
Juniperus communis 'Stricta'		Irish Juniper	616
Juniperus conferta 'Blue Pacific'		Shore Juniper	617
Juniperus horizontalis		Juniper Prostrata	618

BOTANICAL NAME	PRONUNCIATION	COMMON NAME (or newer botanical name)	PLATE NUMBER
Juniperus horizontalis 'Bar Harbor'		Bar Harbor Juniper	619
Juniperus horizontalis 'Variegated'		Juniper Prostrata Variegated	620
Juniperus horizontalis 'Wiltoni'		Wilton Carpet Juniper	621
Juniperus sabina 'Arcadia'		Arcadia Juniper	622
Juniperus sabina 'Broadmoor'		Broadmoor Juniper	623
Juniperus sabina 'Buffalo'		Buffalo Juniper	624
Juniperus sabina 'Tamariscifolia'		Tamarix Juniper or Tam Juniper	625
Juniperus scopulorum 'Blue Haven'		Blue Haven Juniper	626
Juniperus scopulorum 'Pathfinder'		Pathfinder Juniper	627
Juniperus squamata 'Meyeri'		Meyer Juniper	628
Juniperus virginana prostrata Silver Spreader'		Silver Spreader Juniper	629
Kalmia latifolia	Kal-mi-a	Mountain Laurel	194
Kerria japonica	Ker-i-a	Japanese Kerria	195
Koelreuteria bipinnata	Kol-ro-te-ri-a	Chinese Flame Tree	443
Koelreuteria paniculata	Kol-ro-te-ri-a	Golden Rain Tree	444
Kolkwitzia amabillis	Kol-kwit-zi-a	Beauty Bush	304
Laburnum watereri 'Vossi'	La-ber-num	Golden Chain Tree	445
Lagerstroemia indica	La-gur-stre-mi-a	Crape Myrtle	305
Lagunaria pattersonii	La-gun-ar-i-a	Sugar Plum Tree	306
Lantana camara	Lan-tan-a	Lantana	196/197
Lantana sellowiana		Trailing Lantana (L. montevidensis)	69
Laurus nobilis	Lau-rus	Grecian Laurel or Grecian Bay	307
Lavandula vera	La-van-du-la	English Lavender	70
Leptospermum laevigatum	Lep-to-sper-mum	Australian Tea Tree	308
Leptospermum laevigatum 'Reevesii'		Dwarf Australian Tea Tree	198
Leptospermum scoparium 'Helene Strybing'		Flowering Tea Tree	199
Leptospermum scoparium 'Keatleyi'		Pink Flowering Tea Tree	309
Leptospermum scoparium 'Ruby Glow'		Red Flowering Tea Tree	200
Leptospermum scoparium 'Snow White'		White Flowering Tea Tree	71
Leucadendron argenteum	Lu-ka-den-dron	Silver Tree	310
Leucophyllum frutescens	Lu-ko-fi-lum	Texas Sage, Senisa	201
Leucothoe catesbaei	Lu-koth-o-e	Rainbow Leucothoe (L. fontanesiana)	72
Libocedrus decurrens	Li-bo-se-drus	Incense Cedar (Calocedrus)	630
Ligustrum japonicum	Li-gus-trum	Japanese Privet	446
Ligustrum japonicum 'Texanum'		Wax Leaf Privet	202
Ligustrum ovalifolium		California Privet	203
Lippia citriodora	Lip-pia	Lemon Verbena (Aloysia triphylla)	204
Liquidambar styraciflua	Lik-wid-am-ber	Sweet Gum	447
Liquidambar stryaciflua 'Burgundy'		Sweet Gum	448
Liquidambar stryaciflua 'Palo Alto'		Sweet Gum	449
Liriodendron tulipifera	Lir-i-o-den-dron	Tulip Tree	450
Liriope muscari	Li-ri-o-pe	Lily Turfs	73
Lonicera hildebrandiana	Lon-is-era	Giant Honeysuckle	551

BOTANICAL NAME	PRONUNCIATION	COMMON NAME (or newer botanical name)	PLATE NUMBER
Lonicera japonica 'Halliana'		Honeysuckle	552
Loropetalum chinense	Lor-o-pet-a-lum		74
Lyonothamnus floribundus	Lyn-o-tha-mus	Catalina Ironwood	451
Magnolia deciduous varieties	Mag-no-lia	Tulip Trees	311
Magnolia grandiflora		Southern Magnolia	452
Magnolia grandiflora 'Russet'		Russet Magnolia	452 A
Magnolia grandiflora 'Samuel Sommer'		Samuel Sommer Magnolia	453
Magnolia grandiflora 'St. Mary's'		St. Mary's Magnolia	454
Mahonia aquifolium	Ma-ho-nia	Oregon Grape	205
Mahonia aquifolium 'Compacta'		Dwarf Oregon Grape	75
Mahonia bealei		Siberian Grape	206
Mahonia lomariifolia		Chinese Holly Grape	207
Mahonia nervosa		Cascades Mahonia	76
Mahonia pinnata		Cluster Mahonia	208
Malus, In Variety	Mal-lus	Flowering Crabapple	455 to 465
Mandevilla 'Alice Du Pont'	Man-de-vil-a	Chile Jasmine	553
Maytenus boaria	May-ten-us	Mayten	466
Melaleuca decussata	Mel-a-lu-ka	Lilac Melaleuca	312
Melaleuca linariifolia		Flaxleaf Paperbark	467
Melaleuca leucadendra		Swamp Tea Tree	468
Melia azedarach 'Umbraculiformis'	Me-li-a	Texas Umbrella Tree	469
Melianthus major	Mel-i-an-thus	Honey Bush	209
Metasequoia glyptostroboides	Met-a-se-kwoi-a	Dawn Redwood	631
Metrosideros tomentosa	Me-tro-si-de-ros	New Zealand Christmas Tree	470
Michelia fuscata	Mi-ke-li-a	Banana Shrub (*M. figo*)	210
Moraea iridioides	Mo-ree-a	Butterfly Iris	77
Morus alba 'Fruitless'	Mor-us	Fruitless Mulberry	471
Murraya exotica	Mur-re-a	Orange Jessamine	211
		(*M. paniculata*)	
Musa ensete	Mu-sa	Banana Tree	313
		(*Ensete ventricosum*)	
Musa maurelii		Red Leaf Banana	314
		(*Ensete maurelii*)	
Myoporum laetum		My-o-por-um	315/472
Myrsine africana	Mer-seen	African Box	212
Myrtus communis	Mer-tus	Common Myrtle	213
Myrtus communis 'Compacta'		Dwarf Myrtle	78
Myrtus ugni		Chilean Guava	79
Nandina domestica	Nan-dy-na	Heavenly Bamboo	214
Nandina domestica 'Nana Compacta'		Dwarf Heavenly Bamboo	80
Nephrolepis exaltata	Ne-fro-lep-is	Boston Sword Fern	175
Nerium oleander	Nee-ri-um	Oleander	215/216/217
Olea europaea 'Mission'	O-le-a	Olive	473
Osmanthus delavayi	Os-man-thus	Delavayi Osmanthus	218
Osmanthus fortunei		Fortunei Osmanthus	316
Osmanthus fragrans		Sweet Olive	219
Osmanthus ilicifolius		False Holly	220
Osmanthus ilicifolius 'Variegatus'		Variegated False Holly	221
Oxydendrum arboreum	Ox-i-den-drum	Sourwood Sorrel Tree	474

BOTANICAL NAME	PRONUNCIATION	COMMON NAME (or newer botanical name)	PLATE NUMBER
Pachysandra terminalis	Pak-i-san-dra	Japanese Spurge	81
Parthenocissus quinefolia	Par-then-o-sis-us	Boston Ivy, Virginia Creeper *(Ampelopsis)*	522
Passiflora jamesonii	Pas-si-flora	Pink Passion Vine	554
Passiflora pfordtii		Passion Vine	555
Pellaea rotundifolia	Pel-lee-a	Round Leaf Fern	176
Pernettya mucronata	Pur-net-tia	Pernettya	82
Phaedranthus	Fe-dran-thus	Bignonia	525
Philadelphus virginalis	Phil-a-del-fus	Mock Orange	222
Philodendron 'Evansii'	Phil-o-den-dron	Outdoor Philodendron	223
Philodendron selloum		Split Leaf Philodendron	224
Phoenix canariensis	Fe-niks	Date Palm	324
Phoenix reclinata		Senegal Date Palm	325
Phoenix roebelenii		Pygmy Date Palm	326
Phormium tenax	For-mi-um	New Zealand Flax	225
Photinia arbutifolia	Foh-tin-i-a	Toyon *(Heteromeles arbutifolia)*	331
Photinia 'Fraseri'		Fraseri Photinia	475/332
Photinia serrulata		Chinese Photinia	333
Picea excelsa	Pi-se-a	Norway Spruce *(P. abies)*	632
Picea excelsa 'Nidiformis'		Nest Spruce	633
Picea excelsa 'Pendula'		Weeping Norway Spruce	634
Picea excelsa 'Pygmaea'		Dwarf Norway Spruce	635
Picea glauca 'Conica'		Alberta Spruce	636
Picea pungens		Colorado Spruce	637
Picea pungens 'Kosteriana'		Koster Spruce	638
Picea pungens 'Moerheimii'		Moerheim Spruce	639
Pieris	Py-er-is	Lily of the Valley Shrub *(Andromeda)*	228
Pieris formosa 'Forrestii'		Chinese Andromeda	227
Pieris japonica		Lily Of The Valley Shrub	228
Pieris japonica 'Flame Of The Forest'		Flame Of The Forest	229
Pieris japonica 'Flamingo Pink'		Pink Lily Of The Valley Shrub	230
Pieris japonica 'Variegata'		Variegated Lily Of The Valley Shrub	231
Pinus aristata	Py-nus	Bristlecone Pine	640
Pinus canariensis		Canary Island Pine	641
Pinus densiflora 'Umbraculifera'		Tanyosho Pine, Table Mountain Pine	642
Pinus halepensis		Aleppo Pine	643
Pinus mugo mughus		Mugho Pine	644
Pinus nigra		Austrian Black Pine	645
Pinus patula		Jelecote Or Mexican Pine	646
Pinus pinea		Italian Stone Pine	647
Pinus radiata		Monterey Pine	648
Pinus strobus 'Nana'		Dwarf White Pine	649

BOTANICAL NAME	PRONUNCIATION	COMMON NAME (or newer botanical name)	PLATE NUMBER
Pinus sylvestris		Scotch Pine	650
Pinus sylvestris 'Fastigiata'		Erect Scotch Pine	651
Pinus thunbergii		Japanese Black Pine	652/653
Pistacia chinensis	Pis-ta-shi-a	Pistachio	476
Pittosporum crassifolium	Pit-tos-por-um	Karo Pittosporum	334
Pittosporum eugenioides		Tarata Pittosporum	335
Pittosporum phillyraeoides		Desert Willow Pittosporum	336
Pittosporum rhombifolium		Diamond Leaf Pittosporum	337
Pittosporum tenuifolium		Tawhiwhi Pittosporum (P. nigricans)	338
Pittosporum tobira		Japanese Pittosporum	232
Pittosporum tobira 'Variegata'		Japanese Variegated Pittosporum	233
Pittosporum tobira 'Wheelerii'		Wheeler's Dwarf Pittosporum	83
Pittosporum undulatum		Victorian Box	339/477
Platanus acerifolia	Plat-a-nus	London Plane	478
Platanus occidentalis		American Sycamore	479
Platanus racemosa		California Sycamore	480
Platycerium alcicornium	Plat-i-se-ri-um	Staghorn Fern	180
Platycerium grande		Staghorn Fern	181
Pleroma grandiflora	Ple-ro-ma	Princess Flower (Tibouchina semidecandra)	340
Plumbago capensis	Plum-ba-go	Cape Plumbago	234
Podocarpus 'Gracilior'	Pod-o-kar-pus	Fern Pine	341/481/654
Podocarpus macrophyllus		Yew Pine	342/655
Podocarpus macrophyllus 'Maki'		Shrubby Yew	343/656
Poinciana gilliesii	Poin-si-a-na	Bird Of Paradise Shrub	235
Polygala dalmaisiana	Po-lig-a-la	Sweet Pea Shrub	84
Polygonum aubertii	Po-lig-o-num	Silver Lace Vine	556
Polystichum angulare	Po-lis-ti-kum	Single Mother Fern	177
Polystichum munitum		Western Sword Fern	178
Polystichum setosum		Japanese Lace Fern	179
Populus nigra 'Italica'	Pop-u-lus	Lombardy Poplar	482
Potentilla fruticosa	Poh-ten-til-la	Cinquefoil	85
Prunus caroliniana	Pru-nus	Carolina Cherry	344
Prunus caroliniana 'Compacta'		Dwarf Carolina Cherry	236
Prunus cerasifera		Flowering Plum	483/484/485/ 486/487
Prunus glandulosa		Flowering Almond	86
Prunus ilicifolia		Holly Leaf Cherry	345
Prunus lyonii		Catalina Cherry	346
Prunus laurocerasus		English Laurel	347
Prunus laurocerasus 'Otto Luykens'		Luykens Laurel	87
Prunus laurocerasus 'Zabeliana'		Zabel Laurel	88
Prunus lusitanica		Portugal Laurel	348
Prunus persica		Flowering Peach	488/489/490
Prunus serrulata		Flowering Cherry	491/499
Pseudotsuga taxifolia	Su-do-su-ga	Douglas Fir	657

BOTANICAL NAME	PRONUNCIATION	COMMON NAME (or newer botanical name)	PLATE NUMBER
Psidium cattleianum	Sid-i-um	Red Strawberry Guava	349
Punica granatum	Peu-ni-ka	Pomegranate	350
Punica granatum 'Nana'		Dwarf Pomegranate	89
Pyracantha coccinea 'Lalandi'	Py-rah-kan-tha	Firethorn	351
Pyracantha fortuneana 'Graberi'		Firethorn	237
Pyracantha 'Santa Cruz'		Santa Cruz Firethorn	90
Pyrus calleryana 'Bradfordi'	Pyr-us	Bradford Pear	500
Pyrus kawakamii		Evergreen Pear	501
Quercus agrifolia	Quer-kus	California Live Oak	502
Quercus coccinea		Scarlet Oak	503
Quercus ilex		Holly Oak	504
Quercus palustris		Pin Oak	505
Quercus suber		Cork Oak	506
Raphiolepis ovata	Raf-i-ol-e-pis	Raphiolepis umbellata	238
Raphiolepis indica 'Ballerina'		Raphiolepis Ballerina	91
Raphiolepis indica 'Clara'		Raphiolepis Clara	92
Raphiolepis indica 'Enchantress'		Raphiolepis Enchantress	93
Raphiolepis indica 'Pink Lady'		Raphiolepis Pink Lady	94
Raphiolepis indica 'Rosea'		Raphiolepis Rosea	95
Raphiolepis indica 'Springtime'		Raphiolepis Springtime	96
Rhamnus alaternus	Ram-nus	Italian Buckthorn	352
Rhamnus alaternus 'Variegata'		Variegated Italian Buckthorn	353
Rhamnus californica		California Coffee Berry	239
Rhapis excelsa	Ray-fis	Lady Palm	327
Rhododendrons	Rho-do-den-dron	Rhododendron	240
Rhus integrifolia	Roos	Lemonade Berry	354
Rhus ovata		Sugar Bush	241
Rhus typhina 'Laciniata'		Staghorn Sumac	242
Rhynchospermum jasminoides	Rink-co-sper-mum	Star Jasmine *(Trachelospermum jasminoides)*	97/557
Ribes sanguineum	Ri-beez	Red Flowering Currant	243
Ribes speciosum		Fuchsia Flowering Gooseberry	98
Ribes viburnifolium		Evergreen Currant	99
Robinia pseudoacacia 'Decaisneana'	Ro-bin-i-a	Pink Locust	507
Romneya coulteri	Rom-ni-a	Matilija Poppy	244
Rosa banksiae lutea	Roh-za	Banksia Rose	558
Rosmarinus officinalis	Ros-ma-ri-nus	Rosemary	100
Rosmarinus officinalis 'Lockwoodii'		Creeping Rosemary	101
Salix babylonica	Say-lix	Weeping Willow	508
Salix matsudana 'Tortuosa'		Corkscrew Willow	509
Sarcococca hookeriana 'Humilis'	Sar-ko-coke-ah	Small Hookeri	102
Sarcococca ruscifolia		Fragrant Sarcococca	245
Saxifraga rubicunda	Sax-si-fray-ga	Saxifraga *(Bergenia cordifolia)*	103
Schinus molle	Shinus	California Pepper Tree	510
Schinus terebinthifolius		Brazillian Pepper Tree	511
Sciadopitys verticillata	Ski-a-dop-i-tis	Umbrella Pine	658
Seaforthia elegans	Se-for-thi-a	King Palm *(Archontophoenix)*	328

BOTANICAL NAME	PRONUNCIATION	COMMON NAME (or newer botanical name)	PLATE NUMBER
Senecio greyii	Sen-ee-si-o	Senecio	104
Sequoiadendron giganteum	Se-kwoi-a-den-dron	Sequoia *(California Big Tree)*	659
Sequoiadendron giganteum 'Pendula'		Weeping Big Tree	660
Sequoia gigantea	Se-kwoi-a	California Big Tree	659
Sequoia sempervirens		Coast Redwood	661
Skimmia japonica	Skim-i-a	Skimmia	105
			105 A
Solandra guttata	So-lan-dra	Cup Of Gold Vine	559
Solanum jasminoides	So-la-num	Potato Vine	560
Solanum rantonnetti		Paraguay Nightshade	561
Sollya heterophylla	Sol-li-a	Australian Bluebell	106
Sorbus aucuparia	Sor-bus	Mountain Ash	512
Spartium junceum	Spar-ti-um	Spanish Broom	246
Spiraea prunifolia	Spi-re-a	Shoe Button Spiraea	247
Spiraea vanhouttei		Bridal Wreath	248
Stenocarpus sinuatus	Sten-o-car-pus	Firewheel Tree	513
Stephanotis floribunda	Stef-a-no-tis	Madagascar Jasmine	562
Sterculia diversifolia	Stur-cu-lia	Bottle Tree *(Brachychiton populneum)*	514
Stranvaesia davidiana	Stran-ve-zi-a	Chinese Stranvaesia	355
Strelitzia nicolai	Stre-lit-si-a	Giant Bird Of Paradise	356
Strelitzia reginae		Bird Of Paradise	107
Sumac	Su-mac	Rhus	242
Syringa persica laciniata	Si-ring-a	Persian Lilac	249
Syringa vulgaris		Common Lilac	250 to 253
Tamarix tetrandra	Tam-a-riks	Tamarisk	357
Taxus baccata	Tax-us	English Yew	662
Taxus baccata 'Fastigiata'		Irish Yew	663
Taxus baccata 'Fastigiata Aurea'		Golden Irish Yew	664
Taxus baccata 'Repandens'		Spreading English Yew	665
Taxus baccata 'Repandens Aurea'		Spreading Golden English Yew	666
Tecoma capensis	Te-koh-ma	Cape Honeysuckle *(Tecomaria)*	358/563
Ternstroemia japonica	Tern-strom-e-a	Ternstroemia	254
Teucrium chamaedrys	Teu-kre-um	Trailing Germander	108
Teucrium fruticans		Brush Germander	255
Thuja occidentalis 'Little Gem'	Theu-ja	Green Globe Arborvitae	667
Thuja occidentalis 'Pyramidalis'		Pyramidal Arborvitae	668
Thuja occidentalis 'Woodwardi'		Woodwardi Aborvitae	669
Thuja orientalis 'Aurea Nana'		Berckmans Arborvitae	670
Thuja orientalis 'Beverleyensis'		Beverly Hills Arborvitae	671
Tibouchina semidecandra	Ti-boo-shy-na	Pleroma Grandiflora	340
Tilia cordata	Til-i-a	Small Leafed Linden	515
Trachelospermum	Tra-ke-lo-sper-mum	Star Jasmine *(Rhynchospermum)*	97/557
Trachycarpus fortunei	Trac-a-car-pus	Chamerops Excelsa	317
Tristania conferta	Tris-ta-nia	Brisbane Box	516

BOTANICAL NAME	PRONUNCIATION	COMMON NAME (or newer botanical name)	PLATE NUMBER
Tristania laurina		Kanooka Box	517
Tupidanthus calyptratus	Tup-i-dan-thus	Umbrella Tree	359
Tsuga canadensis	Tsu-ga	Canadian Hemlock	672
Tsuga canadensis 'Sargenti'		Weeping Hemlock	673
Ulmus glabra 'Camperdownii'	Ul-mus	Camperdown Elm	518
Ulmus parvifolia		Evergreen Elm	519
Ulmus parvifolia 'Brea'		Chinese Evergreen Elm	520
Vaccinium ovatum	Vak-sin-i-um	Wild Huckleberry	256
Veronica		Hebe	56 to 61
Viburnum burkwoodii	Vi-ber-num	Burkwood Viburnum	360
Viburnum davidii		David Viburnum	109
Viburnum japonicum		Japanese Viburnum	361
Viburnum macrocephalum 'Sterile'		Chinese Snowball	362
Viburnum odoratissimum		Sweet Viburnum	363
Viburnum opulus 'Sterile'		Snowball	364
Viburnum suspensum		Sandankwa	257
Viburnum tinus 'Robustum'		Roundleaf Laurestinus	365
Vitis	Vi-tis	Cissus	536
Washingtonia filifera	Wash-ing-to-nia	California Fan Palm	329
Washingtonia robusta		Mexican Fan Palm	330
Weigela florida	Wi-ge-la	Red Weigela	258
Weigela florida 'Bristol Ruby'			
Weigela florida 'Rosea'		Pink Weigela	259
Westringia rosmariniformis	West-ring-ga	Australian Rosemary	110
Wisteria floribunda	Wis-ta-ri-a	Japanese Wisteria	564
Wisteria sinensis		Chinese Wisteria	567
Wisteria venusta		Silky Wisteria	568
Woodwardia chamissoi	Wood-war-di-a	Giant Chain Fern (W. fimbriata)	183
Xylosma senticosa	Zi-los-ma	Xylosma	260
Yucca aloifolia	Yuk-a	Spanish Bayonet	366
Yucca gloriosa		Spanish Dagger	367
Yucca recurvifolia		Spineless Yucca (Y. gigantea)	368
Zelkova serrata	Zel-ko-va	Sawleaf Zelkova	521

LOW GROWING SHRUBS.
Plants in this section seldom reach over four feet and are easily kept under that height. All are evergreen unless otherwise mentioned.

1   Acanthus mollis

2   Acer palmatum 'Dissectum'

Acanthus mollis   Zone 8

(Bear's Breech)

1   Huge, notched, dark green leaves often two feet long. The leaves grow directly out of the ground, like a perennial, rather than a shrub. Rigid, erect, three-foot flower spikes with whitish or purple-tinged flowers in May and June. Very tropical looking. Stands abuse. Best grown in semi-shade where roots can be confined as they travel underground and are hard to eradicate. The old leaves should be cut to the ground as soon as it finishes blooming. Planting Group 1.

Acer palmatum 'Dissectum'   Zone 5

2   Deciduous foliage comes out red then turns to a rusty green in summer. Shade in warmer areas, but will grow in the sun when the roots are kept shaded and moist but will not tolerate wind. Requires a regular watering schedule.   Planting Group 5

> *Acer palmatum* 'Dissectum' is listed among low-growing plants as it is seldom grown over 4 feet tall. However the above plant, now about 100 years old and with ideal conditions is ten feet. Given time and excellent conditions, most plants will grow taller than expected.

3   Acer palmatum 'Dissectum Everred'

4   Acer palmatum 'Dissectum Viridis'

Acer palmatum 'Dissectum Everred'   Zone 5

3   Deciduous. Same weeping form as the above type except this holds its beautiful deep red color throughout the summer if regularly watered and kept away from wind.   Planting Group 5

Acer palmatum 'Dissectum Viridis'   Zone 5

(Japanese Green Lace Leaf Maple)

4   Deciduous foliage and form the same as the above except it stays bright apple green throughout the summer. Requires regular water and more shade than other varieties of A. palmatum and no wind.
Planting Group 5

5. *Agapanthus africanus*

6   *Agapanthus africanus* 'Peter Pan'

Agapanthus africanus 'Peter Pan'   Zone 8

6   Excellent small dwarf form of the popular "Lily of the Nile" with small clusters of blue flowers on stems about twelve inches tall. There is also a dwarf white form. Deer proof.   Planting Group 1

Agapanthus africanus (A. umbellatus)   Zone 8
(Blue Lily of the Nile)

5   A hardy perennial, producing dense masses of dark green amaryllis-like leaves, and bearing clusters of lovely blue flowers on tall, naked stalks in the summer. Will stand the "impossible" location in full sun. A white form, A. A. Alba is also available. Deer proof.
                                                        Planting Group 1

7   *Agave attenuata*

Agave attenuata   Zone 9

7   Huge rosette of large, thick, fleshy, gray-green leaves. From the succulent family and tropical in effect with very unusual flowers.
                                                        Planting Group 1

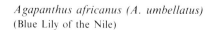

8   *Andromeda polifolia*

Andromeda polifolia   Zone 2
(Bog Andromeda or Bog Rosemary)

8   Dwarf evergreen shrublet to ten inches with gray-green foliage and covered with pink blossoms in the spring. Needs a well-drained but moist place in your garden with an acid soil situation. Best in coastal Northern California or in the Northwest.   Planting Group 1

Arctostaphylos densiflora 'Howard Mc Minn'   Zone 9

9   Leaves are small, one-half to one inch and light to dark glossy green. Flowers are whitish pink. Will grow to about thirty inches in height with a six-foot spread. Best planted with afternoon shade or an eastern exposure. Tip prune after blooming for tight dense growth. Needs a well-drained location and do not water too much. Deer proof.   Planting Group 3

10   *Arctostaphylos hookeri*

Arctostaphylos hookeri   Zone 7

(Monterey Manzanita)

10   Grows to about two feet with a four to five-foot spread. Leaves are shiny bright green and has pinkish flowers. Excellent cover for dry slopes. Deer proof.   Planting Group 2

9   *Arctostaphylos densiflora* 'Howard McMinn'

Arctostaphylos uva ursi   Zone 2

(Kinnikinnick or Bearberry)

11   A creeping Manzanita with rich green leaves that grow only a few inches high. The plants take root as they spread. Should be planted at about three-foot centers. Flowers are white followed by red berries. Widely planted, especially near the coast and in the Northwest.
                                                     Planting Group 2

11   *Arctostaphylos uva ursi*

Aspidistra elatior   Zone 9

(Cast Iron Plant)

12   Excellent both in a tub (or indoors) or planted in the garden as a specimen. One of the most rugged plants for a tough dark location. Very good as an indoor specimen.   Planting Group 5

12   *Aspidistra elatior*

AZALEAS

Now referred to by botanists as Rhododendrons. However, in this book, we are calling them Azaleas because this is the way they are described in the wholesale nursery catalogues. They are unsurpassed for blooms in winter and spring. They are all lovers of acid soil and do best when planted in peat moss or leaf mold with excellent drainage. They all like partial shade or morning sun and plenty of water, however, the Southern Indicas or Sun Azaleas will grow in full sun if they do not receive reflected heat. Feed as soon as the blooming is over and while the plant is in active growth. Prune, even with hedge shears, in May or June to shape the plant for compact growth.

Sun Azaleas   Zone 9

SOUTHERN INDICAS — Hardy to about 25 degrees.

Brilliant	single red
Duc De Rohan	single salmon pink
Fielder's White	single fragrant white
Formosa	single rich lavender
George L. Tabor	large single pink
L. J. Bobbink	single pinkish lavender
Glory of Sunnyhill	single orange red
Southern Charm	single deep rose
Pride of Dorking	single cardinal red

Kurume Azaleas   Zone 8

The Kurume strain blooms in the late spring. The plants are hardier in the garden than the Indicas, both to cold and in their capacity to stand more sun. The flowers are not so large as the Indicas, but are more profuse. Again, dozens of varieties to be found and we only attempt to list a few:

Coral Bells	single bright pink, stands sun
Hexe	deep red hose-in-hose
Hino (Hinodegiri)	single bright red, stands sun
Hino Crimson	single crimson, stands sun
Sherwood Orchid	single orchid, stands sun
Sherwood Red	single red, stands sun
Sweetheart Supreme	double light pink
Red Wing	single ruffled red, large
Ward's Ruby	single brilliant dark red

Planting Group 5

Azaleas for the shade   Zone 9

Belgian indicas or closely related varieties best above twenty-five degrees. The choicest of all the Azaleas. Mostly double flowers in a great range of colors. Listed below are some of the most readily available:

Alaska	double white
Albert and Elizabeth	double white with pink edging
Avenir	double salmon
Blushing Bride	large, double soft pink blooms
California Snow	large, double, white
California Sunset	large, double, salmon and white variegated
Chimes	large, double, red
Dr. Bergman	varied shades of pink, rose and salmon
Pink Dr. Bergman	light pink
Erie (Eric Schame)	variegated pink and white double
Fred Sanders	large, double, rose red
Jean Hearrens	large, double, lavender pink
Niobe	large, double, pure white
Orchidiflora	extra large, double, lavender pink
Paul Schame	double, coral salmon
Pearl De Sweynarde	large double white
Picotee	large variegated white with pink edge
Pink Pearl	large double, delicate pink
Rose Queen	hose-in-hose pink
Vervaeneana Alba	large double pure white
William Van Orange	double orange

Planting Group 5

AZALEAS

If you want to treat your Azaleas right when you plant them, dig a hole three feet in diameter and six inches deep even for a one-gallon can size, larger if the plant has a larger root ball. Fill this hole with seventy-five percent peat moss and twenty-five percent loose loam or compost, as most Azaleas are grown in pure peat in California and will not send their roots out into heavy soil.

Treat your Azaleas to the best. In dry weather use a prepared wetting agent once a month which will force the peat moss to accept water.

13-A   *Azalea altaclarensis*

13-B   *Azalea Exbury hybrids*

Azalea altaclarensis   Zone 5

(Chinese Azalea)

13-A   Deciduous. Resembles A. Mollis except in color. This variety has large flowers of apricot yellow in varying tones and grows to about six feet. Same growing instructions as A. Mollis.   Planting Group 1

Azalea Exbury hybrids   Zone 6

13-B   Deciduous. There are many named varieties but, for the most part, nurseries carry seedling plants by color only. Red, orange, pink, and white. These beautiful plants grow in more sun than most other Azaleas and are upright in growth to about five feet. Should have a loose, sandy peaty soil that is mounded up around the stems.

Planting Group 1

13-C   *Azalea mollis*

> The latest botanical books list all Azaleas as Rhododendrons; however, we are calling the plants by the name that they are sold under at the leading wholesale nurseries. This not only applies to Azaleas but to the other plants listed throughout the book.

Azalea mollis   Zone 6

13-C   Deciduous to six feet. The flowers, borne in large clusters, are bright orange to flame, also yellow and white. Best grown in full sun on the coast. Partial shade inland in a well-drained, well-watered location. Likes acid soil, so plant with leaf mold and peat moss. The plant does best when planted in a mound like a hill of potatoes, with peat moss and leaf mold mixture.   Planting Group 1

Azalea occidentalis   Zone 7

(Western Azalea)

13-D   Deciduous. Has delightful, fragrant, showy, tubed-shaped flowers in rounded clusters. The flowers, borne in May and June, vary in color from white to cream to pinkish. Grows to about six feet, but occasionally to ten feet or more.   Planting Group 4

13-D   *Azalea occidentalis*

13E Azalea 'Sweatheart Supreme'   *13F Azalea* 'Mission Bell'

13G Azalea 'Rose Queen'   *13H Azalea* 'Southern Charm'

13I Azalea 'California Sunset'   *13J Azalea* 'Memorie Jean Hearrens'

13K Azalea 'Erie (Eric Schame)'   *13L Azalea* 'Dr. Bergman'

13M Azalea 'Sherwood Red'   *13N Azalea* 'Iveryana'

13O   *Azalea* 'Red Wing'

13P   *Azalea* 'George Tabor'

13Q   *Azalea* Garden

13R   *Azalea* 'Ward's Ruby'

13S   *Azalea* 'Coral Bells'

13T   *Azalea* 'Hino Crimson'

13U   *Azalea* 'Ledifolia Rosea'

13V   *Azalea* 'L.J. Bobbink'

13W   *Azalea* 'Mamie'

13X   *Azalea* 'Duc De Rohan'

14 *Bambusa sasa* 'Pygmaea'

15 *Beloperone guttata*

Bambusa sasa 'Pygmaea'   Zone 9
(Dwarf Bamboo)

14 Excellent to use where a low-growing plant or ground cover is desired but travels and can become a pest. However, planting in a confined area is helpful. Golden-green foliage. Also available in a silver variegated form.   Planting Group 1

Beloperone guttata (B. tomentosa)   Zone 9
(Shrimp Plant)

15 Dwarf shrub with attractive, long, reddish-brown bracts that hide a small white flower. Likes heat, takes full sun, but does best in partial shade with good drainage.   Planting Group 1

16 *Bouvardia albatross*

Bouvardia albatross   Zone 9
(White Bouvardia)

16 A shrub noted for its fragrant, showy clusters of white flowers. Tender. To develop a nice plant, it is necessary to pick the flowers with a short stem regularly. Grow in partial shade with mixtures of peat moss and leaf mold. Use acid fertilizer. Because it is a victim of smog, not readily available.

          Planting Group 5

Buxus japonica   Zone 8
(Japanese Boxwood)

17 Popular, quick-growing, low hedge or shrub. Foliage medium to light green. Usually kept clipped to a height of two to three feet, but will grow to six feet or more if untrimmed.   Planting Group 1

17 *Buxus japonica*

18   *Buxus sempervirens* 'Suffruticosa'

19   *Calluna vulgaris* 'H.E. Beale'

21   *Carissa grandiflora* 'Tuttleii'

Buxus sempervirens 'Suffruticosa'   Zone 7
(Dwarf English Boxwood)

18   This "true" dwarf variety is widely used in the Northwest and Northern California. Ideal for a low evergreen border to be kept at one to two feet. Requires closer planting than the Japanese boxwood.   Planting Group 1

Many varieties of Calluna Vulgaris, the true Scotch Heather, are grown in the Northwest. We only show two. These are very simular to some of the Ericas shown later in this book.

Calluna vulgaris 'H.E. Beale'   Zone 4
(Scotch Heather)

19   A very colorful loose mound to two feet with dark green needle-like foliage and soft pink double flowers on long spikes which are good for cutting. Needs a well drained soil.   Planting Group 1

Calluna vulgaris 'Searlei'   Zone 4

20   Another of the many varieties of the Heaths grown on the Pacific Coast, mostly in the Northwest. This one has white flowers and blooms in the late summer and fall in a well drained area.
                                                    Planting Group 1

20   *Calluna vulgaris* 'Searlei'

Carissa grandiflora 'Tuttleii'   Zone 9
(Dwarf Natal Plum)

21   This knee-high dwarf form of C. Grandiflora has the same lush green foliage as the parent with abundant white flowers which are followed by red fruit. Excellent ground cover to control unwanted foot traffic; there are just enough thorns.   Planting Group 1

Ceanothus griseus horizontalis   Zone 8
(Carmel Creeper)

23   Very popular in the coastal region. The leaves are bright green and about two inches long. The plant is covered in spring with light blue flowers. Plants grow eighteen to thirty inches high, and will cover the ground within a year, if growing conditions are right. For ground cover, should not be planted closer than five or six-foot centers, otherwise the plants will mound up.   Planting Group 2

22   Ceanothus gloriosus

Ceanothus gloriosus   Zone 8
(Point Reyes Creeper)

22   Low-growing, dense met, usually about six or eight inches high. The foliage is small, spiny, and dark green with medium blue flowers. Very good when planted on top of a wall hanging straight down. One of the best Ceanothus ground covers when planted three to four-foot centers.   Planting Group 2

23   Ceanothus griseus horizontalis

24   Ceratostigma plumbaginoides

Ceratostigma plumbaginoides   Zone 8
(Blue Leadwort)

24   Ground cover plant with intense blue flowers in summer and fall. Looks sad in winter so should be cut back to the ground in late fall. Spreads from underground roots. Will grow in sun on the coast but prefers shade inland. Flowers freely in the shade.   Planting Group 1

Cistus corbariensis   Zone 8
(White Rock Rose)

25   Another wonderful cover for dry, sunny slopes either in the desert or right next to the ocean. Plant is very compact and has two-inch white flowers. Must have dry, well-drained location. Deer proof.   Planting Group 3

26   Cistus ladaniferus 'Maculatus'
Cistus ladaniferus 'Maculatus'   Zone 8
(Crimsonspot Rock Rose)

26   Compact growth to three feet high with glossy green leaves and three-inch white flowers with a crimson spot on each petal. Flowers heavily in June and July. Will stand salt spray or hot desert and enjoys poor soil. Will also stand drought conditions and is an excellent bank cover. Deer proof.   Planting Group 3

25   Cistus corbariensis

27   *Cistus purpureus*

28   *Clivia miniata*

Cistus purpureus   Zone 8
(Orchid Rock Rose)

27   Compact growth up to four or five feet with dark green foliage. Flowers are orchid with a dark eye. Enjoys drought, poor soil, ocean breeze, but is equally at home in the hot country. Deer proof.
                                        Planting Group 2

Clivia miniata   Zone 9
(Kafir Lily)

28   Large, deep green, lily-like shaped leaves. Bright orange flower clusters in late winter or early spring. Needs shade and no direct sun. Excellent tub plant for shade as it likes confinement.
                                        Planting Group 5

Convolvulus cneorum   Zone 9
(Bush Morning Glory)

29   A very nice, low-growing, silver-gray plant that should be planted in full sun. Tends to be leggy in the shade. white flowers similar to morning glory (it is of the same family) all summer. Gray foliage means that it will not stand too much garden water.
                                        Planting Group 3

29   *Convolvulus cneorum*

31   *Coprosma kirkii*

30   *Coprosma baurei* 'Aurea'

Coprosma baurei 'Aurea' *(C. repens variegata)*   Zone 9
(Trailing Variegated Coprosma)

30   An excellent rapid-growing ground cover. Best near the coast. The dark green leaves shine like a mirror and have greenish-yellow blotches. Grows to about three feet.   Planting Group 1

Coprosma kirkii   Zone 9

31   A low-growing, spreading, small-leaf variety of the mirror plant used as a ground cover or as a very low shrub. Excellent bank cover, especially near the coast.   Planting Group 1

Correa pulchella   Zone 9
(Australian Fuchsia)

32 An excellent, low-growing, compact shrub to two feet that is
covered from mid-winter through spring with dainty, pink, tubular
flowers about one inch long. Grows in the sun and like so many
of the plants from Australia, it requires excellent drainage and only
small amounts of water.   Planting Group 3

33 *Cotoneaster dammeri*

Cotoneaster dammeri   Zone 7
(Bearberry Cotoneaster)

33 Grows only six inches high and forms a dense mat that will hang
straight down over a wall. Bright green foliage about one inch long.
White flowers, red berries.   Planting Group 1

32 *Correa pulchella*

35 *Cotoneaster horizontalis*

Cotoneaster horizontalis   Zone 4
(Rock Cotoneaster)

35 Flat, spreading shrub that loses its foliage in the winter but it
is never missed because the plant is so heavily covered with bright-red
berries. Good in sun or shade. Very effective as a low divider to stop
traffic, or as a mass ground cover.   Planting Group 1

34 *Cotoneaster glaucophylla*

Cotoneaster glaucophylla   Zone 5
(Gray Leafed Cotoneaster)

34 Low, bushy plant with small, gray-green foliage and bright-red
berries. Excellent low-growing shrub for a dry area.
                                                     Planting Group 2

Cotoneaster microphylla   Zone 4
(Rockspray Cotoneaster)

36 A low-growing one-foot evergreen with tiny foliage and rose-red
berries that hold all winter. Excellent bank cover. Planting Group 1

36 *Cotoneaster microphylla*

37   Cyperus alternifolia

39   Daphne odora 'Marginata'

Daphne odora 'Marginata'   Zone 8
(Winter Daphne)

39   A superior, dense, low shrub with gold-margined leaves and small clusters of intensely fragrant, pink and white flowers. Tempermental around San Francisco, but blooms well elsewhere. Full sun in the cooler areas, but shade where it is warm. Blooms January to March. Needs excellent drainage and should be planted higher or on a slight mound to prevent "collar rot".   Planting Group 5

41   Deutzia gracilis

Cyperus alternifolia   Zone 9
37   Reed-like stems headed with fine feathery foliage resembling a palm. Thrives best in a moist spot. Will grow in shallow water such as a fish pond. Sun or shade.   Planting Group 1

Daphne cneorum   Zone 6
(Rock Daphne)

38   Low evergreen, growing nine to twelve inches and spreading two to three feet. Small, gray-green foliage one inch long, and covered with fragrant, pink flowers in April or May. Recommended for the Northwest, but not too good in California, where it must be top dressed with peat and loam after bloom to prevent dieback.
                                                          Planting Group 1

38   Daphne cneorum

40   Daphne burkwoodii 'Somerset'

Daphne burkwoodii 'Somerset'   Zone 4
40   Evergeen to about zero degrees, then semi-evergreen in the colder areas. Erect, compact growth to about four feet with closely-set narrow leaves and small clusters of fragrant pink flowers. Needs excellent drainage, even a raised bed.   Planting Group 2

Deutzia gracilis   Zone 6
41   Deciduous. Graceful, two to four-foot shrub with an abundance of pure-white flowers in the spring.   Planting Group 1

44   *Equisetum hyemale*

43   *Diosma ericoides*

Diosma ericoides (D. reevesi or Coleonema album)   Zone 9
(Breath of Heaven or Baby's Breath)

43   Taller growing than the pink variety, with arching branches. Excellent landscape shrub to lighten the effect of a heavy, solid shrubbery line. Masses of small white flowers. Should be kept pruned to three feet.   Planting Group 1

Diosma pulchrum (Coleonema pulchrum)
Zone 9

(Pink Breath of Heaven)

42   A dwarf, compact, bushy shrub with heather-like foliage, and masses of tiny pink flowers during spring and summer. Should be pruned heavily after blooming. Sun.
Planting Group 1

42   *Diosma pulchrum*

Equisetum hyemale   Zone 9
(Horsetail Reed Grass)

44   A rush-like deep green tropical grass with jointed stems. Excellent for tropical effect but should be contained. Requires abundant water; even grows in a shallow fish pond.   Planting Group 1

Erica carnea 'Springwood White' and   Zone 5
'Springwood Pink'

45-46   Delightful early spring-blooming shrubs to about one foot tall. Sometimes used as a bank ground cover. There are many varieties used and grown mostly in the Northwest but are available sometimes in Northern California. The plants need excellent drainage and never should be allowed to dry out.   Planting Group 2

45   *Erica carnea* 'Springwood Pink'

46   *Erica carnea* 'Springwood White'

47   *Eriogonum arborescens*

Eriogonum arborescens   Zone 9
(Wild Buckwheat)

47   Narrow gray foliage on a bush that grows two to four feet across. Flowers are pink, in long flat clusters that may be dried for flower arrangements. Stands winds and fog, but must have good drainage. Not too good inland.   Planting Group 3

Euryops pectinatus   Zone 9

48   An evergreen perennial that blooms almost the year around. Yellow daisy flowers and gray-green foliage. Drought resistant and thrives even in ocean winds.   Planting Group 1

48   *Euryops pectinatus*

50   *Gardenia jasminoides* 'Mystery'

49   *Festuca glauca*

Festuca glauca   Zone 8
(Blue Fescue)

49   Hardly a shrub, but an attractive, ornamental blue grass, which grows in small clumps to six inches. Excellent small plant for borders or edging. Widely used for "Oriental" garden effects.
                     Planting Group 2

FERNS

All ferns are listed together in the medium section regardless of height.

Gardenia jasminoides 'Mystery'   Zone 8
(Cape Jasmine)

50   A handsome three to four-foot shrub with large, fragrant white flowers, ideal for corsages. Should be planted in soil composed of sand, peat and leaf mold. Must have perfect drainage. Should not be cultivated. Feed regularly with blood meal, and if leaves are still yellow, try iron sequestrene. Best where there is heat. Do not plant in full shade.   Planting Group 2

Gardenia jasminoides 'Veitchi'   Zone 8

52   Smaller blooms than Gardenia Mystery, but blooms more profusely and over a longer period. Needs feeding regularly and if leaves
turn yellow, add iron and mulch with leaf mold and peat. Best in
the warmer valleys. Requires excellent drainage.   Planting Group 2

51   Gardenia jasminoides 'Radicans'

52   *Gardenia jasminoides* 'Veitchi'

Gardenia jasminoides 'Radicans'   Zone 8

51   A low form of Gardenia that grows only a foot tall. Has miniature
Gardenia flowers about the size of a silver dollar. A beautiful little
rock plant, but, like the two other Gardenia varieties described, difficult to raise. For most people, it will either grow nicely or not at
all. If you like Gardenias, it is worthwhile trying. Requires good drainage.   Planting Group 2

53   *Gaultheria procumbens*

54   Gaultheria shallon

Gaultheria procumbens   Zone 3
(Wintergreen)

53   Excellent ground cover with a creeping habit forming a mat of
dark fragrant waxy green foliage which turns bronze in the fall. White
flowers in the spring and large red berries in the fall. Needs very
well drained soil.   Planting Group 1

Gaultheria shallon   Zone 5
(Salal or Lemon Leaf)

54   Native to coastal areas from Santa Barbara to British Columbia.
The cut branches are collected in the wild and sold by florists as
"lemon leaves". Will grow in poor soil and with neglect to about
two feet but in good garden conditions, in the shade, to over four
feet. White or pinkish flowers in clusters in the spring and edible
black fruit in the fall.   Planting Group 1

Grevillea noelli   Zone 9

55   A clean, low, compact plant with needle-like bright green foliage
and rose-red blooms in the spring. Excellent bank cover.
                                                   Planting Group 1

55   *Grevillea noelli*

56   Hebe buxifolia

58   Hebe 'Evansi'

Hebe 'Evansi' *(H. rubra or Veronica rubra)*   Zone 9

58   The leaves are a blend of dark green and reddish-purple, about two inches long. Flowers are three inches and reddish-purple. Blooms in summer.   Planting Group 1

60   Hebe menziesii

Hebe buxifolia *(Veronica buxifolia)*   Zone 9

56   Low, compact shrub with small one-half inch long leaves, and small, white flowers. Very useful for low edging or a globe-shaped plant. All Hebes stand heavy pruning.   Planting Group 1

57   Hebe 'Co-ed'

Hebe 'Co-ed' *(Veronica co-ed)*   Zone 8

57   One of the newer varieties and one of the best. A compact bush with rich, dark green leaves and purplish-pink flowers borne in profusion during spring and summer. Like all Hebes does better in coastal areas than the hot interior.   Planting Group 1

59   Hebe imperialis

Hebe imperialis *(Veronica imperialis)*   Zone 8

59   Compact, rounded shrub to four feet. Clean, glossy-green foliage, one to three inches long and reddish-purple flower spikes. Good coastal plant. Stands heavy pruning.   Planting Group 1

Hebe menziesii *(Veronica menziesii)*   Zone 9

60   A small, shiny-leafed, compact plant with arching branches and a profusion of small, showy white flowers. Best in the cool, coastal areas and in the shade.   Planting Group 4

61   *Hebe* 'Patty's Purple'

62   *Helleborus lividus corsicus*

Hebe 'Patty's Purple' (*Veronica* 'Patty's Purple')   Zone 8

61   A small variety usually not more than eighteen inches tall. Very nice for compact borders. Purple flowers in spring and summer.

Planting Group 1

Helleborus lividus corsicus   Zone 8
(Corsican Hellebore)

62   Excellent perennial to two feet with blue green leaves with sharply toothed edges. Clusters of large chartreuse flowers. Flowers in late fall and winter in Southern California but in the Northwest they arrive in March and April. Best in partial shade.   Planting Group 4

Hypericum calycinum   Zone 5
(Aaron's Beard)

63   Excellent groundcover to one foot in height. Bright yellow flowers in the spring or summer, either in full sun or partial shade. Spreads by underground runners and once established will grow without too much water. It can be hard to control in a garden.

Planting Group 1

63   *Hypericum calycinum*

Hypericum moserianum   Zone 8
(Gold Flower)

64   A delightful low foundation plant with arching branches to three feet in height. Golden yellow flowers in spring and summer. Stands full sun or partial shade on the coast, but does best in partial shade in the interior.   Planting Group 1

64   *Hypericum moserianum*

Hypericum patulum henryii   Zone 7
(St. John's Wort)

65   A nice, evergreen shrub to four feet tall, with continuous yellow blooms all summer. Stands pruning. Grows in any soil, sun or partial shade. Seldom looks like much in a container at the nursery, but develops into a wonderful plant in the garden.   Planting Group 1

65   *Hypericum patulum henryii*

66   Ilex cornuta 'Rotunda'

67   Ilex crenata 'Green Island Holly'

***Ilex cornuta* 'Rotunda'**   Zone 6
(Dwarf Japanese Holly)

66   Compact, low-growing holly with dense habit of growth. Ideal for both sun or shade. Does not produce berries but is a valuable landscape plant for its excellent habits and abundance of attractive, shapely leaves.   Planting Group 1

***Ilex crenata* 'Green Island Holly'**   Zone 6

67   An excellent low growing small leaved plant that is so dense it looks very much like a boxwood and can be used the same way. Usually grows to twenty four inches in a nice tight mound but can be trimmed as a hedge. Sun or part shade and usually found in the Northwest.   Planting Group 1

Jasminum magnificum (J. nitidum)   Zone 10
(Angel Wing Jasmine)

68   A small, evergreen, semi-vining spreading shrub. Large shiny green leaves and glistening fragrant white flowers. Planting Group 1

68   Jasminum magnificum

69   Lantana sellowiana

Lantana sellowiana (L. montevidensis)   Zone 9
(Trailing Lantana)

69   Lavender flowers on a low, fast-spreading plant, seldom over one foot, unless it can climb. Likes heat and dry soils. Planting Group 2

70   Lavandula vera

Lavandula vera   Zone 7
(English Lavender)

70   Attractive, gray-green, compact shrub with fragrant lavender spikes of flowers in the spring.   Planting Group 3

Leucothoe catesbaei 'Rainbow'　　　Zone 5
(Leucothoe fontanesiana)

(Drooping Leucothoe)

72　Evergreen shrub to about three or four feet. Is related to the Andromeda family. The leathery leaves have a bronze tint in the winter and clusters of white flowers. Does best in woodland gardens with deep soil.　　　Planting Group 1

72　*Leucothoe catesbaei* 'Rainbow'

71　*Leptospernum scoparium* 'Snow White'

Leptospernum scoparium 'Snow White'　　　Zone 9

71　A spreading compact plant to about four feet with needle-like foliage and medium-sized double white flowers with greenish centers. Flowers all spring usually starting in December.　Planting Group 3

73　*Liriope muscari*

Loropetalum chinense　　　Zone 4

74　Usually this plant is a three to four foot shrub but sometimes taller. Neat, compact habit with drooping branches. Flowers are white to greenish white in clusters at the end of branches. Heavy bloom in March and April with some blooms all summer. Full sun in cooler areas to partial shade inland. Needs well drained soil with ample water.　　　Planting Group 4

Liriope muscari　　　Zone 6

73　Dark green, grass-like leaves form clumps to twelve to eighteen inches and produce spikes of lavender flowers. Best in partial shade.　　　Planting Group 4

74　*Loropetalum chinense*

Mahonia aquifolium 'Compacta'　　　Zone 5

75　The same handsome evergreen foliage and the same rich yellow clusters of flowers as the regular Oregon Grape, except it only is one-third the size, usually not over two feet.　Planting Group 4.

75　*Mahonia aquifolium* 'Compacta'

76   *Mahonia nervosa*

78   *Myrtus communis* 'Compacta'

79   *Myrtus ugni*

Myrtus ugni   Zone 8
(Chilean Guava)

79   Attractive, bushy shrub for partial shade in the valley, full sun on the coast. Rounded foliage less than one inch long. Small white flowers in the spring and edible, reddish fruits in the fall. Likes slightly acid soil and should not be allowed to dry out. Never a good-looking plant when young in a container, but well worthwhile when older. The edible fruit is delightful.   Planting Group 1

Mahonia nervosa   Zone 5
(Longleaf Mahonia)

76   Native from Northern California to British Columbia. A low-growing species with long slender leaves. Full sun or deep shade. Yellow flowers in the spring. Usually two to three feet but will grow to six feet in excellent soil.   Planting Group 1

77   *Moraea iridioides*

Moraea iridioides   Zone 8
(Butterfly Iris)

77   Narrow iris-like foliage with stalks of white iris-like flowers having yellow and blue markings, bloom only when the sun shines. The flowers close up at night.   Planting Group 1

Myrtus communis 'Compacta'   Zone 8
(Compact Myrtle)

78   Small leaves densely massed on this compact shrub. Excellent for low hedges, either trimmed or untrimmed. Fragrant foliage.
                                                                 Planting Group 1

80   *Nandina domestica* 'Nana Compacta'

81 *Pachysandra terminalis*

82 *Pernettya mucronata*

Pernettya mucronata   Zone 7

82 Compact evergreen shrub to about three feet with small glossy dark green foliage. Small, pinkish bell-shaped flowers in the spring followed by very colorful berries. Each plant a different color berry: red, pink, white or purple. Grow in acid, peaty soil with ample water. Sun in cooler areas and part shade in warmer areas.
Planting Group 5

Nandina domestica 'Nana Compacta'   Zone 6

80 More compact than Nandina Domestica. Usually not more than eighteen inches. Same fine green lacy foliage but somewhat heavier than the regular Nandina and turns a spectacular red in the fall, especially in areas with lots of warm weather.   Planting Group 1

Palms

All palms are listed together in the tall shrub section.

83 *Pittosporum tobira* 'Wheelerii'

Pachysandra terminalis   Zone 5
(Japanese Spurge)

81 A low-growing, six-inch bright, glossy green, creeping plant, spreading by underground runners. Give it a rich soil on the acid side with plenty of moisture. Best in shade as it tends to yellow in the sun. Stands light traffic.   Planting Group 4

Pittosporum tobira 'Wheelerii'   Zone 8
(Wheeler's Dwarf)

83 Excellent low-growing mound shrub with the same shiny green foliage of Pittosporum Tobira. Requires very little maintenance. Use as a low mound or a low round hedge. Seldom over two feet tall.
Planting Group 1

Polygala dalmaisiana   Zone 9
(Sweet Pea Shrub)

84 Small evergreen, ever-blooming shrub to three feet. Small, gray-green leaves and quantities of pea-shaped orchid flowers. Good drainage required. Needs full sun.   Planting Group 2

84 *Polygala dalmaisiana*

85   *Potentilla fruticosa var* 'Katherine Dykes'

Potentilla fruticosa var. 'Katherine Dykes'   Zone 3

85   Low, mounding shrub with lemon-yellow flowers borne in profusion all summer. Attractive gray-green foliage. It is deciduous and will grow in poor soil, in heat, and with little water. Many other varieties available, from bright yellow to white.   Planting Group 1

87   *Prunus laurocerasus* 'Otto Luykens'

89   *Punica granatum* 'Nana'

Prunus glandulosa   Zone 4
(Dwarf Flowering Almond)

86   Deciduous, small, upright, heavily-branched shrub to about four feet. Varieties available are double pink and double white, blooming in January or February. Needs heavy pruning each year and can be pruned while in flower, or shortly after.   Planting Group 1

86   *Prunus glandulosa*

Prunus laurocerasus 'Otto Luykens'   Zone 8

87   A compact, low-growing, wide-spreading, very hardy laurel with dark green glossy foliage. White flower spikes on the branches in the spring.   Planting Group 1

88   *Prunus laurocerasus* 'Zabeliana'

Prunus laurocerasus 'Zabeliana'   Zone 7
(Zabel Laurel)

88   A valuable spreading evergreen shrub. The leaves are smaller and more pointed than English Laurel. Will grow to five or six feet, but can easily be kept under three feet by removing branches that grow up. The color is a good, bright green and the plant is very tolerant of different types of soil and sun and shade conditions.
          Planting Group 1

Punica granatum 'Nana'   Zone 8
(Dwarf Pomegranate)

89   A dwarf, compact, bushy shrub. Produces single vivid orange-red flowers in abundance. It is deciduous and of ornamental value only. Likes sun and heat.   Planting Group 1

Pyracantha 'Santa Cruz'   Zone 8

90   Excellent as a ground or a bank cover with low growth and a spreading habit. The foliage is much denser than P. Yunnanensis and berries are large and dark red, borne in huge clusters.
Planting Group 1

90   Pyracantha 'Santa Cruz'

91   Ralphiolepis 'Ballerina'

Raphiolepis 'Ballerina'   Zone 8

91   One of the more compact varieties of this wonderful group. Seldom more than two feet high and about five feet across. The flowers are a deeper shade of pink than most of the varieties available in the trade.   Planting Group 1

93   Raphiolepis indica 'Enchantress'

92   Raphiolepis indica 'Clara'

Raphiolepis indica 'Clara'   Zone 8

92   This white-flowered form is a compact three to four-foot plant. Like the rest of the Raphiolepis, this is a full sun plant but will take a good amount of shade.   Planting Group 1

Raphiolepis indica 'Enchantress'   Zone 8

93   Another excellent plant that is easily kept under two feet. Pink flowers in profusion and a very compact plant. Flowers the same as 'Springtime'.   Planting Group 1

Raphiolepis indica 'Pink Lady'   Zone 8

94   One of the most popular varieties of all. This handsome shrub grows to about four feet, either in full sun or in part shade. Similar to Springtime in foliage and color of flowers.   Planting Group 1

94   Raphiolepis indica 'Pink Lady'

95   *Raphiolepis indica rosea*

96   *Raphiolepis indica* 'Springtime'

97   *Rhynchospermum jasminoides*

Raphiolepis indica rosea   Zone 8
(Pink India Hawthorne)

95   A neat, low-growing evergreen shrub with bright, shiny, green foliage. Soft pink flowers cover the bush in the spring and then bloom to a lesser degree all summer. Blue berries, in clusters in fall and winter. Will sometimes grow taller than four feet, but will stand pruning and should be kept under that height.   Planting Group 1

Raphiolepis indica 'Springtime'   Zone 8

96   This very attractive shrub is a beauty from February to May with a profusion of pink blooms. Like the other Raphiolepis, the shrub has glossy, leathery leaves and will stand heavy pruning. Full sun or part shade.   Planting Group 1

Rhynchospermum jasminoides   Zone 9
(*Trachelospermum jasminoides*)
(Star Jasmine)

97   Although this is a vine, we are listing it here because it is often sold as a shrub to be grown into a low mound or ground cover. It is one of our finest evergreen vines. Does equally well in sun or shade. The flowers from May to July are very fragrant, especially in the evening. Also used as a ground cover, but it is not for dry banks as it must have water and a moist location.   Planting Group 1

   Many varieties of Raphiolepis are grown in the West, all slightly different. To list a few: R. Apple Blossom, R. Bill Evans, R. Coates Crimson, R. Flamingo, R. Jack Evans, R. Pink Cloud, Pinkie, and others.

98   *Ribes speciosum*

Ribes speciosum   Zone 9
(Fuchsia Flowering Gooseberry)

98   Native shrub along the coast from Baja California to San Fransisco. Erect growing to three or four feet with spiney stems on thick green leaves and deep crimson, fuchsia-like flowers with long stamens. Likes partial shade and is an excellent barrier.   Planting Group 3

Ribes viburnifolium   Zone 8
(Evergreen Currant)

99 A California native evergreen shrub with a habit of growth that
calls for ground cover use. It is spreading, half-trailing, and roots
where it touches ground. The flowers are light pink to rose from
February to April. Sun or partial shade on the coast, part shade inland.   Planting Group 1

100   Rosmarinus officinalis

99   *Ribes viburnifolium*

Rosmarinus officinalis   Zone 7
(Rosemary)

100 Used since ancient times for cooking. Small, narrow, dark,
gray-green, aromatic foliage and light blue flowers. This plant requires
full sun, poor soil and almost no water at all.   Planting Group 2

102   Sarcococca hookeriana 'Humilis'

Sarcococca hookeriana 'Humilis'   Zone 7

102 Growth very low and spreading from underground roots. The
flowers are very small, white and fragrant. One of the best for low
planter boxes in complete shade, or partial shade. Likes a loose, leaf
mold soil and acid food.   Planting Group 4

101   *Rosmarinus officinalis* 'Prostrata'

Rosmarinus officinalis 'Prostrata'   Zone 6
(R. O. Lockwoodii)
(Trailing Rosemary)

101 A dwarf shrub about six to twelve inches tall with deep grayish-
green, fragrant foliage. The clusters of flowers are light blue. This
plant enjoys poor soil and lack of water. A very dry bank is ideal,
however, it is not recommended for people with hayfever, asthma,
or an allergy to bees.   Planting Group 2

Saxifraga rubicunda (Bergenia cordifolia)   Zone 8
(Saxifrage)

103 A compact, perennial evergreen plant with large, round, dark
green leaves and clusters of pink flowers in early spring. Recommended
for planter boxes in front of stores where the going is tough. A "tropical
effect" ground cover. Likes some shade.   Planting Group 1

103   *Saxifraga rubicunda*

104   Senecio greyii

Senecio greyii   Zone 7

104   One of the most handsome gray plants, and like almost all gray plants, needs only minimum amounts of water and a well-drained soil. Grows to three, sometimes four feet in full sun. Leaves leathery, gray-green with silver edge.   Planting Group 3

Sollya heterophylla   Zone 9
(Australian Blue Bell)

106   Evergreen, half shrub, half vine with masses of brilliant blue one-half-inch bells through most of the summer. Full sun or part shade on the coast, part shade inland. Very satisfactory ground cover.   Planting Group 3

106   Sollya heterophylla

105   Skimmia japonica — Female

Skimmia japonica — Female   Zone 5

105   Slow growing, low shade plant. In California, it needs special attention to soil condition. Use peat, leaf mold, and sand. Grows where Azaleas grow. Male plants are needed for pollination and grow taller. Female plants produce clusters of holly-like, bright red berries. Best in mass planting.   Planting Group 4

105-A   Skimmia japonica — Male

Skimmia japonica — Male   Zone 5

105-A   This plant grows taller than the female and is needed for pollinization. The heavy spring bloom makes this a desirable plant even without the females close by. Skimmia should not be allowed to dry out during the summer.   Planting Group 4

107   Strelitzia reginae

108   Teucrium chamaedrys

Strelitzia reginae   Zone 9

(Bird of Paradise)

107   Exotic orange, blue and white "birds" on stiff stems. Plants do best in rich, well-drained soil and react favorably to acid food. Full sun on the coast, part shade inland.   Planting Group 1

Teucrium chamaedrys   Zone 7

(Dwarf germander)

108   Low evergreen shrub with glossy leaves and reddish-purple flowers. Plant in full sun in a well-drained soil. It thrives in a hot, dry location and will rot in a heavy, wet soil.   Planting Group 3

109   Viburnum davidii

Viburnum davidii   Zone 7

109   This low-growing evergreen has deeply-creased large leaves that densely cover the plant. Clusters of white flowers in June followed with light blue berries. Best in the Northwest or in the cooler parts of Northern California.   Planting Group 5

Westringia rosmariniformis   Zone 9

(Australian Rosemary)

110   An Australian shrub known as Victorian Rosemary. Wind tolerant and drought resistant. Rosemary-like leaves light gray-green in color, and small white flowers in the spring borne in profusion (all year in the milder climates). Needs a light, well-drained soil in the sun.   Planting Group 3

110   Westringia rosmariniformis

MEDIUM GROWING SHRUBS

Plants described in this group usually grow from four to eight feet or are usually kept pruned to this height. All plants evergreen unless otherwise mentioned.

112   Abelia grandiflora

111   Abelia 'Edward Goucher'

Abelia 'Edward Goucher'   Zone 6
(Pink Abelia)

111   Graceful, arching branches of bronzy foliage, laden with lavender-pink, bell-shaped flowers throughout the summer. Sun or shade.   Planting Group 1

Abelia grandiflora   Zone 6
(Glossy Abelia)
112   Graceful evergreen shrub with fragrant, white, bell-shaped flowers in spring and summer. The rich, dark green foliage turns to bronze and then to red as soon as the cold weather comes. An old standby in landscaping.   Planting Group 1

Abutilon hybrids   Zone 9
(Flowering Maple)

113   Medium-sized, upright shrub with arching branches holding bell-like flowers. Various colors: red, yellow and white, etc. Very attractive to hummingbirds.   Planting Group 4

113   Abutilon hybrids

116   Aralia sieboldii

Aralia sieboldii   Zone 9
(Fatsia japonica or A. japonica)
(Glossy Aralia)

116   Excellent for tropical effects in shade; however, it will take all
but the hottest sun. In the sun it loses its luster and becomes yellowish.
Makes a wonderful tub plant when planted in clumps of three or
four.   Planting Group 1, best in 5

Arbutus unedo 'Compacta'   Zone 7
(Compact Strawberry Tree)

117   A much more compact form of Arbutus
Unedo. Foliage somewhat smaller. Very colorful
and attractive. Deer proof.   Planting Group 1

117   Arbutus unedo 'Compacta'

114   Althaea, Rose of Sharon

Althaea (Hibiscus syriacus)   Zone 5
(Rose of Sharon)

114   Deciduous. Grown extensively in the
colder climates, it is hardy to zero but loves
the warm climate of the interior. Wide color
range: red, rose, purple, blue, and white, both
single and double flowers.   Planting Group 1

115   Aralia elegantissima

Aralia elegantissima   Zone 10
(Dizygotheca elegantissima)
(False Aralia)

115   An unexcelled evergreen shrub with deep
green, heavily-serrated leaves. If given good
light when young it turns a deep bronze-purple
with smaller leaves. Ideal indoor plant in a
bright area.   Planting Group 2

118 *Aucuba japonica*

121 *Aucuba japonica* 'Variegata'

Aucuba japonica 'Variegata' Zone 7
(Gold Dust Plant)

121 Male and female of the most widely used Aucubas which flourish in full or partial shade with plenty of water. The gold-specked foliage is four to six inches long and two to three inches wide. Stands heavy pruning, but usually grows only about twelve to eighteen inches a year and to about six feet. Female plants produce large red berries when planted with male varieties. Named male plants not too plentiful in most nurseries. Planting Group 4

Aucuba japonica Zone 7
(Dwarf Aucuba)

118 Bright red berries on this tropical-appearing four to five-foot plant. The foliage is shiny dark green and like the rest of the Aucubas it is an excellent plant for a shady area. It needs a male plant nearby to pollenize it for berry production. Planting Group 4

119 *Aucuba japonica* 'Crotonifolia'

Aucuba japonica 'Crotonifolia' Zone 6

119 Another outstanding Aucuba. This one is a male plant with brightly-colored leaves that does wonders for a shady garden when mixed with other Aucubas to induce berries. It likes only a little sun. Like most of the other Aucubas, this one grows to about six feet and can stand heavy pruning. Planting Group 4

Aucuba japonica 'Picturata' Zone 7

120 Large bright golden leaves with a green edge. Very showy. Like the rest of the Aucubas this one likes the shade and will grow with little care. (Female.) Planting Group 4

120 *Aucuba japonica* 'Picturata'

122 *Berberis darwinii*

125 *Brunfelsia calycina* 'Floribunda'

Berberis darwinii   Zone 3
(Darwin Barberry)

122 One of the showiest of the Barberries, it bears masses of small, holly-shaped, dark green leaves. Clusters of orange-yellow flowers in spring, followed by dark blue berries. It will grow higher, but should be kept under six feet.   Planting Group 1

Berberis julianae   Zone 7
(Wintergreen Barberry)

123 Evergreen to semi-deciduous. Very leathery, spiny-toothed, three inch long dark green leaves with reddish fall color. Formidable as a barrier hedge, as this is one of the thorniest. Grows to six feet.
                          Planting Group 1

123 *Berberis julianae*

Berberis thunbergi 'Atropurpurea'   Zone 3
(Red Leaf Japanese Barberry)

124 Deciduous. Leaves are reddish purple when planted in the sun but green in the shade. Excellent low four to five-foot hedge, or as a mass planting with thorns where no traffic is wanted. B. Thunbergi, the green variety, is also available.   Planting Group 1

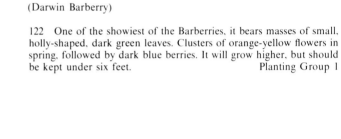

Brunfelsia calycina 'Floribunda'   Zone 8
(Yesterday, Today and Tomorrow Shrub)

125 Compact shrub grows to five feet in shade or part sun. The interesting common name comes from the white flowers (yesterday), bright blue fragrant flowers (today), and blue buds (tomorrow), all showing at the same time. Best in rich, slightly acid, well-drained soil. Long blooming period.   Planting Group 4

124 *Berberis thunbergi* 'Atropurpurea'

128 *Calliandra tweedii*

127 *Calliandra inequilatera*

Calliandra inequilatera   Zone 9
(Pink Powderpuff)

127 Medium sized tropical evergreen shrub. Lots of bright pink stamens that look like a huge powder puff which contrasts with the rich, green foliage.   Planting Group 2

Calliandra tweedii   Zone 9
(Brazilian Flame Bush)

128 Leaves are lacy and fern-like. Each branch bears medium-sized heads of fluffy, vivid scarlet stamens, shaped like pom-poms. Blooms all spring and summer.
                    Planting Group 2

Buxus sempervirens   Zone 5
(English Boxwood)

126 Tall growing; usually used as a trimmed pyramid, in globes, or in a hedge.
                    Planting Group 1

PLANTING GUIDE

Following each description is a planting group guide. Here again, individual conditions will vary so the planting instructions are general. An attempt has been made to give you a clue to the general soil conditions needed for each plant. You should check local conditions with your nurseryman.

Group 1 means the plant will grow in the sun without special treatment, unless otherwise mentioned.

Group 2 means the plant will grow in the sun, but must have excellent drainage.

Group 3 means the plant will grow in the sun, but must have excellent drainage and only minimum amounts of water, usually gray foliage plants.

Group 4 means the plant will grow in the shade, without special treatment.

Group 5 means the plant will grow in the shade, but must have excellent drainage and special soil mixture.

TEMPERATURE RATINGS

Zone 10	40° to 30°
Zone 9	30° to 20°
Zone 8	20° to 10°
Zone 7	10° to 0°
Zone 6	0° to -10°
Zone 5	-10° to -20°
Zone 4	-20° to -30°
Zone 3	-30° to -40°

Temperatures suggested in this book are approximate. The growing conditions, for example, a warm late fall often will keep the plants from hardening off and a sudden cold snap has been known to freeze plants 20° above the normal freezing point.

126 *Buxus sempervirens*

CAMELLIAS

Truly the aristocrat of all garden plants. No other group of plants (except roses) commands the attention that this lovely group does. Here again we are listing all Camellias in the medium group, knowing full well they will grow higher in time, however from a landscape point of view, six to eight feet is the height that most varieties can be kept with a minimum of pruning.

They grow best with an eastern exposure, or full shade in the hot interior, with a soil rich in humus and peat moss and in a moist and well-drained location. Avoid planting any deeper than grown in the nursery and avoid a poorly-drained location. Best when heavily mulched, especially in the warmer interior. If planting in a sunny location, place the plant so the leaves shade the soil (even a slight tilt) or place a good-sized boulder or two in front to keep the sun off the ground.

129   *Camellia japonica* 'Grandiflora Rosea'

130   *Camellia japonica* 'Kumasaka'

CAMELLIA JAPONICA

ADOLPHE AUDUSSON SPECIAL	red and white
ALBA PLENA	double white
BELLA ROMANA	light pink striped carmine
BETTY SHEFFIELD SUPREME	white, rose border
BLOOD OF CHINA	deep salmon-red
CARTER'S SUNBURST	pale pink, rose striped
CHANDLERI ELEGANS	rose-pink and white
C.M. WILSON	light pink
DAIKAGURA	bright rose-pink and white
DEBUTANTE	light pink
DRAMA GIRL	salmon rose-pink
E.G. WATERHOUSE	formal pink
ELEANOR HAGOOD	pale pink
ELENA NOBILE	flame red
FIMBRIATA ALBA	white, fringed petals
FINLANDIA VARIEGATED, (Margaret Jack)	white and crimson
FINLANDIA	white
FRANCINE	rose pink
GLEN 40	deep red
GRANDIFLORA ROSEA	deep pink
GUILIO NUCCIO VARIEGATED	coral rose pink and white
HERME (Jordan's Pride)	pink, deep pink stripes with white edge
KRAMER'S SUPREME	rich red
KUMASAKA	rose pink
LALLAROOK (Laurel Leaf)	pink and white
MAGNOLIAEFLORA	blush pink
MATHOTIANA, (Julia Drayton)	crimson
MATHOTIANA ALBA	white
PEARL MAXWELL	shell pink
PINK PERFECTION	shell pink
POPE PIUS IX	cherry red
PROF. CHARLES S. SARGENT	dark red
PURITY	white
SHIRO CHAN	white

SASANQUA CAMELLIAS

APPLE BLOSSOM	white bluish pink
JEAN MAY	shell pink
SHOWA NO SAKAE	soft pink
SHOWA SUPREME	soft pink
SPARKLING BURGUNDY	ruby rose
TANYA	deep rose pink
WHITE DOVES	white
YAE ARARE	white
YULETIDE	orange-red, yellow stamens

130A   Camellia japonica 'Eleanor Hagood'

130C   Camellia japonica 'Grandiflora Rosea'

130D   Camellia japonica 'Villa de Nantes'

130E   Camellia japonica 'Finlandia Variegated'

130G   Camellia japonica 'Chandleri Elegans'

130H   Camellia japonica 'Mrs. Charles Cobb'

130I   Camellia japonica 'Glen 40'

130J   Camellia japonica 'Mrs. D.W. Davis'

130K   Camellia japonica 'Mathotiana Alba'

130L   Camellia japonica 'Kramer's Supreme'

130M   Camellia japonica 'Shiro Chan'

130N   Camellia japonica 'C.M. Wilson'

130O   Camellia reticulata 'Crimson Robe'

130P   Camellia reticulata 'Brigadoon'

130Q   Camellia reticulata 'Cornelian'

130R   Camellia sasanqua 'Jean May'

130S   Camellia sasanqua 'Shishi-Gashira'

130T   Camellia sasanqua 'Setsugekka'

132   Cassia artemisioides

131   Carissa grandiflora

Cassia artemisioides   Zone 9
(Wormwood Senna)

132   Attractive, light-textured shrub, three to four feet tall. Gray foliage with light yellow flowers during winter and spring. Like most other gray foliage plants, it requires very good drainage.
Planting Group 3

Carissa grandiflora   Zone 9
(Natal Plum)

131   A round shrub to about five or six feet with glossy foliage. Often used as an attractive and useful informal hedge. The thorns will discourage traffic, and the shiny, red fruit looks like a plum, but tastes much better.
Planting Group 2

Ceanothus impressus   Zone 8
(Santa Barbara Ceanothus)

133   Low growing, (about five feet high), with spreading small, crinkly dark green foliage. The deep blue flowers are quite large. One of the best.
Planting Group 2

Ceanothus 'Julia Phelps'   Zone 8

134   Rich, cobalt blue flowers that are fairly small but in dense clusters. The plant is garden tolerant and grows to six or seven feet in height with a ten foot spread. When in bloom the intense blue color is stunning. One of the best steep hillside plants.
Planting Group 2

133   Ceanothus impressus

Ceanothus 'Mountain Haze'   Zone 8

135 The foliage is dark green with small, soft blue flowers in April and May. One of the best garden varieties in the four to six-foot class. Will stand pruning.   Planting Group 2

Cestrum parqui   Zone 9
(Night Blooming Jasmine)

136 Just an ordinary green shrub by day with small, greenish-yellow flowers, but at night one of the most strikingly fragrant shrubs in the trade. Often freezes to the ground but comes back up in the spring. Best as a five to seven foot shrub. Needs heavy cutting to keep it in hand. Does best in warmer climate.   Planting Group 1

135 Ceanothus 'Mountain Haze'

134 Ceanothus 'Julia Phelps'

136 Cestrum parqui

Chamaelaucium ciliatum (C. uncinatum)   Zone 9
(Geraldton Wax Flower)

137 Medium to tall-growing shrub that should be kept pruned to a maximum of six feet. It has light green, needle-like foliage, and sprays of light pink to white flowers of a waxy appearance. The flowers last for a long time. Full sun and excellent drainage required.   Planting Group 3

138 Choisya ternata

Choisya ternata   Zone 8
(Mexican Orange or Mexican Mock Orange)

138 A very useful and desirable three to five-foot shrub for sun or shade. Foliage is rich green, and heavy. Fragrant flowers borne in orange blossom-like clusters. Will turn yellow immediately if drainage is poor.   Planting Group 2

137 Chamaelaucium ciliatum

141   *Citrus* 'Tangerine'

139   *Citrus* 'Meyer Lemon'

Citrus 'Meyer Lemon *(C. limon "Meyeri")*   Zone 9
(Dwarf Meyer Lemon)

139   One of the best dual-purpose plants in the trade today. Dwarf in habit. Good, bold green foliage; constantly covered with fragrant white flowers, and plenty of ripe fruit most of the year. Requires good drainage, regular fertilization and full sun. Water sparingly, but deeply.   Planting Group 2

142   *Citrus* 'Kumquat'

140   *Citrus* 'Grapefruit'

143   *Coprosma baueri*

Citrus   Zone 9

140-141-142   Many varieties are available and if you are fortunate enough to live in a warm area, try one near the front door, especially one grown on dwarf understock. Bright shiny leaves, fragrant flowers and attractive fruit. Only a few of the many varieties are pictured.   Planting Group 3

144   *Cordyline stricta*

145   *Corokia cotoneaster*

Coprosma baueri   Zone 9
(Mirror Plant)

143   Excellent shrub in the coastal area. Leaves are round, shiny and green. Will grow taller than six feet, but it should be pruned to below that height. In coastal areas, it will grow in full sun, shade inland. One of the few plants that will grow (and look good) under that "unsightly deck".   Planting Group 1

146   *Corylus avellana contorta*

Cordyline stricta   Zone 9
(Palm Lily)

144   A fine container plant, indoors or outdoors. Excellent tropical-effect plant in a sunny location near the coast or in the shade in the desert. This plant will grow to ten feet, but may be kept narrow and much smaller.   Planting Group 5

Corylus avellana contorta   Zone 4
(Walking Stick)

146   Branches on this twisted filbert make a very unusual display. A fantastic container plant that will grow to seven or eight feet but best when kept around four feet.   Planting Group 1

Corokia cotoneaster   Zone 8
(Cotoneaster corokia)

145   Slow growing to seven or eight feet, but usually kept in the four-foot range. Delightful branch pattern made up of almost black, thin, contorted branches. Very dark, three-quarter-inch leaves that are dusty white underneath; hundreds of tiny bright yellow flowers in the spring. Excellent tub plant that tolerates sun or part shade but needs fast-draining, alkaline soil.   Planting Group 2

Crassula argentea   Zone 9
(Jade Plant)

147   Excellent house plant or outdoor container plant as well as an excellent landscape plant in a mild climate. This succulent has fleshy leaf pads one to two inches long and lovely pink flowers in early spring.   Planting Group 1

147   *Crassula argentea*

148   Crataegus contorta

Crataegus contorta   Zone 5
(Snake Hawthorne)

148   A unique twisted form of Crataegus that makes an excellent
bonsai both in a pot or in the garden. Small double-red flowers similar
to C.O. Paul Scarlet. Usually found in the Northwest.
                                                     Planting Group 1

149   Crotalaria agatiflora

150   Cydonia japonica

Crotalaria agatiflora   Zone 8
(Canary Bird Bush)

149   The flowers are chartreuse. A great favorite among flower
arrangers. The foliage is gray-green and the one-and-one-half inch
flowers are in clusters for a foot or more along the stem. Grows in
full sun and should be pruned and thinned regularly.
                                                     Planting Group 2

Cydonia japonica (Chaenomeles japonica)   Zone 5
(Flowering Quince)

150   Deciduous. Winter flowering in red, white and pink. The flowers
are excellent for flower arrangement. The shrub makes a wonderful
untrimmed hedge if you have enough room. The thorns will stop
all traffic. A number of varieties are available in most nurseries.
                                                     Planting Group 1

Cytisus   Zone 6
(Scotch Broom)

Small to medium size shrubs with tiny bright green leaves. Flowers
in early spring when long sprays of blooms appear along the branches.

Burkwoodi
Deep red blooms, upright. Not shown.

Hollandia
151   Purplish red blooms, upright.

Kewensis
153   Cream white flowers, dwarf spreading.

Lydia
152   Yellow flowers, spreading, prostrate habit. Blooms late.

Moonbeam
154   Glowing moonbeam yellow.

Peter Pan
Red blooms, dwarf growing. Not shown.

Praecox
155   Creamy yellow flowers on arching branches.

St. Mary's
Snow-white blooms, upright growth. Not shown.

152 Cytisus Lydia

151 Cytisus Hollandia

153 Cytisus Kewensis

154 Cytisus Moonbeam

155 Cytisus Praecox

156   Daubentonia tripetii

158   Erica melanthera rosea

Daubentonia tripetii Zone 8
(Scarlet Wisteria Tree)

156   Deciduous. A fast growing shrub to seven or eight feet with wide, lacy leaves. Showy, burnt orange clusters of pea-shaped flowers reminiscent of Wisteria. Contrary to its common name, it is neither a tree, nor a Wisteria, nor scarlet. Short lived. Planting Group 1

Erica melanthera rosea Zone 9
(Pink Scotch Heather)

158   A tall shrub with long plumes of pink flowers during the winter. Should be pruned for the flowers during, or right after, flowering to a four or five foot height, but will grow higher. Grows in sun or partial shade. Requires a very well-drained, peat or sandy acid soil. Planting Group 2

157   Echium fastuosum

Echium fastuosum Zone 9
(Pride of Madeira)

157   Large, four to five foot clumps of gray-green, narrow leaves on a rounded mound. Large, delphinium-like spikes of blue-purple flowers (up to three feet above the plant), give a bold effect. Good at the seashore or dry location and enjoys poor soil.
 Planting Group 2

Erica melanthera rubra Zone 9
(Red Scotch Heather)

159   A compact shrub of medium height with dark green, needle-like foliage. The flowers come on the new wood in long plumes of deep pink in the late fall. The shrub should be cut back to encourage new growth after blooming. Requires a peat loam soil on the acid side and very good drainage. Planting Group 2

159   Erica melanthera rubra

160   Escallonia rubra

161   Eugenia myrtifolia 'Compacta'

Escallonia rubra   Zone 8
(Red Escallonia)

160   A medium-sized bush five to six feet high, that will grow in sun or shade and stand any amount of pruning. Flowers are red in nice clusters with shiny, glossy, green background foliage. Stands seashore conditions.
                                        Planting Group 1

162   Euonymus alata

Eugenia myrtifolia compacta   Zone 9
(*Syzygium paniculatum compacta*)

161   Dwarf form of E. Myrtifolia on which the new foliage stays red for a longer period of time. With little effort it can be kept at any point in the three to six-foot range and can be shaped.   Planting Group 1

Euonymus alata   Zone 3
(Burning Bush)

162   A compact, deciduous shrub that grows slowly to five feet and is a must in the colder areas; this one has foliage that turns the most brilliant red of any garden shrub.
                                        Planting Group 1

163   Euonymus japonica

Euonymus japonica   Zone 5
(Evergreen Euonymus)

163   Good, slow growing, compact shrub for foundation planting. Most of the Euonymus family are inclined to mildew in coastal areas, but are excellent in the hot interior.   Planting Group 1

165   *Euonymus japonica aureo variegata*

164   *Euonymus japonica aureo marginata*

166   *Euonymus japonica silver queen*

Euonymus japonica aureo marginata
Zone 5

(Golden Euonymus)

164   Green leaves with golden edges.
Planting Group 1

Euonymus japonica aureo variegata
Zone 5

(Gold Spot Euonymus)

165   On this outstanding variety leaves are gold in the center with dark green edges.
Planting Group 1

Euonymus japonica silver queen   Zone 5
166   Large evergreen foliage. Metallic green leaves with creamy white margins.
Planting Group 1

TEMPERATURE RATINGS

Zone 10	40* to 30*
Zone 9	30* to 20*
Zone 8	20* to 10*
Zone 7	10* to 0*
Zone 6	0* to -10*
Zone 5	-10* to -20*
Zone 4	-20* to -30*
Zone 3	-30* to -40*

Temperatures suggested in this book are approximate. The growing conditions, for example, a warm late fall often will keep the plants from hardening off and a sudden cold snap has been known to freeze plants 20* above the normal freezing point.

FERNS

There is a fern for practically any shady or partially shady spot in the garden. All ferns require good drainage and must have a soil rich in humus. The softness ferns bring to the garden is worth the extra care they require.

All ferns are listed together in the medium section regardless of height.

167   Adiantum pedatum

168   Alsophila australis

Adiantum pedatum   Zone 4
(Five Finger Fern)

167   Native in the cooler areas along the Pacific Coast, often growing in the wild on banks where the water is dripping or excellent pot plant in a shaded garden bed.   Planting Group 5

Alsophila australis (A. cooperi)   Zone 9
(Australian Tree Fern)

168   A beautiful tree fern with a slender, graceful trunk and a crown of spreading five to eight-foot fronds. A fast grower that needs shade and regular moisture.   Planting Group 5

169   Asparagus 'Meyerii'

Asparagus 'Meyerii'   Zone 9
169   Stiff upright stems to two feet that are densely clothed in needle-like, deep green leaves which have a fluffy look. A very interesting plant both in the garden or as a hanging basket.   Planting Group 5

Asparagus ferns are not ferns but are listed with ferns because they are commonly referred to as ferns.

170   Asparagus sprengerii

Asparagus sprengerii   Zone 9

170   Small leaves on long, arching branches, making a mound of green foliage. Prefers shade, but will grow in considerable sun on the coast. Extensively used in hanging baskets and as an indoor plant.
Planting Group 5

171   Aspidium capense

Aspidium capense   Zone 9
(Leather Leaf Fern)

171   The triangular fronds are a deep glossy green, firm textured and excellent for flower arrangements. Best in partial shade to two feet, but will grow in full sun in some areas.   Planting Group 5

172   Asplenium bulbiferum

Asplenium bulbiferum   Zone 9
(Mother Fern)

172   Exotic, long, light green fronds, which remind one of carrot leaves. The new fern is produced in the axil of its fronds. Prefers shade. Grows to two feet.   Planting Group 5

173   Cyrtomium falcatum

174   Dicksonia antartica

175   *Nephrolepis exaltata*

176   *Pellaea rotundifolia*

Cyrtomium falcatum   Zone 8
(Holly Fern)

173   A coarse, holly-like leaf with stiff dark green fronds to two feet.
Prefers shade.   Planting Group 5

Dicksonia antartica   Zone 9
(New Zealand or Tasmanian Tree Fern)

174   Hardiest of the tree ferns. Will take sun on the coast and is
excellent as a tub plant. Has a dark brown trunk with a heavy crown
of feathery fronds, often as many as fifty. Much more compact than
the other tree ferns, so more desirable for the small garden.
                                            Planting Group 5

Nephrolepis exaltata   Zone 9
(Boston Sword Fern)

175   The upright Boston Sword fern grows in the coastal areas in
Zone 9 and in many places in full sun. Vigorous grower and divides
easily. Usually not more than thirty inches.   Planting Group 5

177   *Polystichum angulare*

Pellaea rotundifolia   Zone 9
(Round Leaf Fern)

176   Small fern with spreading fronds to one foot. The leaflets are
evenly spaced and about three-fourths of an inch across. Filtered
shade.   Planting Group 5

Polystichum angulare   Zone 8
(Single Mother Fern)

177   Low growing fern with spreading, lacy fronds which are covered
with small plantlets that reproduce readily. Excellent rock garden
plant.   Planting Group 5

Polystichum munitum   Zone 7
(Western Sword Fern)

178   Native to our Pacific coast. Grows in a clump with two or three
foot fronds and is best when naturalized on a woody hillside.
                                            Planting Group 5

178   *Polystichum munitum*

179   Polystichum setosum

Polystichum setosum   Zone 8
(Japanese Lace Fern)

179   Splendid low growing fern with handsome, lacy, dark green
foliage usually about one foot tall.   Planting Group 5

180   Platycerium alcicorne

181   Platycerium grande

Platycerium alcicorne   Zone 9
(Staghorn Fern)

180   The most common of the staghorn group. The gray-green fronds
are thick and clustered, usually to fifteen or eighteen inches long but
sometimes to three feet. In nature, they grow on trees, and here, they
often escape the bark slab they are started on. Excellent plant for
a shaded patio. Staghorn ferns are usually grown on a slab of wood or
bark and hung on a wall or tree.

Platycerium grande   Zone 9
(Staghorn Fern)

181   Very broad fronds resembling moose antlers but somewhat
divided. Fertilize with blood meal or fish emulsion at the back of
each clump. Excellent patio "talking piece" but must be protected
from frosts below 27 degrees. Do not overwater.

182   Woodwardia chamissoi

Woodwardia chamissoi (W. fimbriata)   Zone 8
(Giant Chain Fern)

182   Upright growth with four to five foot fronds. Stands considerable
sun, is excellent background plant for partially shaded areas. Gives
a tropical appearance.   Planting Group 5

FUCHSIAS

Zone 9

There is no better place in the world to grow Fuchsias than the San Francisco Bay Area and along the California coast one-hundred miles north and south. In the forty years I have been connected with the nursery industry, I have seen over one-thousand varieties in the trade. No attempt will be made to describe any varieties. Enough to say that there are low-growing, drooping varieties; low-growing uprights; medium-growing uprights; and tall-growing uprights. They carry, in each kind, small flowers, large flowers, single flowers and double flowers in many colors.

Planting Group 5

182   Fuchsia

183   Fuchsia

184A   Fuchsia 'Al Stettler'

184B   Fuchsia 'Sincerely'

184C   Fuchsia 'Keepsake'

184E   Fuchsia 'Psychedelic'

184D   Fuchsia 'Happy Talk'

184H   Fuchsia 'Belvedere'

184F   Fuchsia

184G   Fuchsia

184I   Fuchsia 'Gartenmeister Bonsted'

185 *Forsythia*

187 *Genista racemosa*

186 *Garrya elliptica*

Forsythia species   Zone 4

185 Deciduous. Forsythia are grown in many varieties in other parts of the country, but on the West Coast, most nurseries carry Forsythia, period. Little regard is shown for the variety name here. Will sometimes grow more than six feet, but normally four to six feet. Long sprays of bright golden flowers from January to March. A bright spot in a winter garden. Excellent for a dramatic bouquet indoors.

       Planting Group 1

Garrya elliptica   Zone 9

(Silk Tassel Bush)

186 A very attractive, hardy, dense, evergreen shrub to five or six feet or more. The interesting and very attractive flowers have pendulous catkins, almost a foot long. Excellent for the seashore.

       Planting Group 3

Genista racemosa   Zone 8

(Sweet Broom)

187 A free-flowering shrub that will grow in any soil. The golden yellow flowers are pea-shaped and often times will reseed themselves.   Planting Group 2

Gunnera chilensis   Zone 8

188 This plant is reminiscent of a giant rhubarb. The leaves are often five feet or more in diameter. Needs soil rich in humus, high in nitrogen, and never let it dry out. Ideal for a bog. Leaves should be cut clear back if not killed by frost. Partial shade.   Planting Group 1

189 *Hibiscus moscheutos*

188 *Gunnera chilensis*

HIBISCUS.

Hibiscus are sunny, warm-weather plants for Zone 10 and high Zone 9. However, many of us consider them "fun plants" and in May, in frost areas, buy a plant and treat it as an annual. In full sun it will bloom every day with usually a dozen blooms at a time and will last until freezing weather comes. The cost of a fine five-gallon-size plant, about the same as you and your wife spend for a nice lunch.

Agnes Gault	The tallest, hardiest, and most popular single pink. Flowers up to six inches in diameter.
Brilliant (San Diego Red)	Single bright red flowers with bright green foliage.
Butterfly	Lemon yellow.
California Gold	Yellow, orange center.
Crown of Bohemia	Double yellow with orange-red throat.
Diamond Head	Large double; deep pink.
Hula Girl	Single, rich yellow with a red throat.
Kona	Full double pink of the same color as Agnes Gault.
Red Monarch	Medium-size plant with a compact habit of growth. Rich crimson double red.
Ross Estey	Large single rose with orange edges.
White Wings	Single white, red throat.

Hibiscus moscheutos   Zone 8
(Rose Mallow, Perennial Hibiscus)

189   Hardy perennial. Stems grow to six or eight feet each year. Starts blooming in late June and continues until frost, then dies down for the winter. Flowers are the largest of all Hibiscus. Some varieties up to twelve inches. Colors white, pink or red. A hot weather plant.
Planting Group 1

190   Hibiscus 'White Wings'

Hibiscus rosa sinensis in variety   Zone 9

190   A very popular shrub but actually somewhat tender for even most of California. In colder areas, with hot summers, we recommend that they be planted as annuals in April or May for the great masses of bloom they will produce all summer. Full sun and good drainage. We list some of the most popular varieties, but there are many more in the trade. Most varieties are in the five to seven-foot class, but some will easily grow to twelve feet in warmer areas of Zone 9.
All Planting Group 1

190A   Hibiscus 'Agnes Gault'

190A-2   Hibiscus 'White Wings'

190B   Hibiscus 'San Diego Red'

190C   Hibiscus 'Kona'

190D   Hibiscus 'Diamond Head'

190E   Hibiscus 'Agnes Gault'

190F   Hibiscus 'Hula Girl'

190G   Hibiscus 'Crown of Bohemia'

190H   Hibiscus 'Ross Estey'

190I   Hibiscus 'Butterfly'

TEMPERATURE RATINGS

Zone 10	40° to 30°
Zone 9	30° to 20°
Zone 8	20° to 10°
Zone 7	10° to 0°
Zone 6	0° to -10°
Zone 5	-10° to -20°
Zone 4	-20° to -30°
Zone 3	-30° to -40°

Temperatures suggested in this book are approximate. The growing conditions, for example, a warm late fall often will keep the plants from hardening off and a sudden cold snap has been known to freeze plants 20° above the normal freezing point.

HYDRANGEA HORTENSIS.

Deciduous. A large growing shrub four to six feet high; covered in early summer with mammoth blooms, some up to one foot in diameter. Best in light shade. Many people make the mistake of cutting their plants down from a five foot plant to two feet during the winter. This delays blossoming until late August. Instead, thin one-third of the plant from the base in order to develop new shoots from the ground. It will then blossom in early June. Not too many nurseries carry named varieties. Some of the named varieties are:

Hamburg	Scarlet
Hortensia	Deep pink
Merritt's Beauty	Carmen red
Revelation	Brilliant red
Trophee	Brilliant salmon rose
White	White

Planting Group 4

191 *Hydrangea*

192 *Hydrangea*

BLUE HYDRANGEAS

There aren't any. What you have seen is the result of a chemical change caused by acid soil. Pink varieties may be changed to blue by adding Iron Sulfate or Aluminum Sulphate to the soil. To keep the pink, add lime. Whites do not change color satisfactorily.

PLANTING GUIDE

Following each description is a planting group guide. Here again, individual conditions will vary so the planting instructions are general. An attempt has been made to give you a clue to the general soil conditions needed for each plant. You should check local conditions with your nurseryman.

Group 1 means the plant will grow in the sun without special treatment, unless otherwise mentioned.

Group 2 means the plant will grow in the sun, but must have excellent drainage.

Group 3 means the plant will grow in the sun, but must have excellent drainage and only minimum amounts of water, usually gray foliage plants.

Group 4 means the plant will grow in the shade, without special treatment.

Group 5 means the plant will grow in the shade, but must have excellent drainage and special soil mixture.

193   Ilex cornuta burfordi

Ilex cornuta burfordi   Zone 7
(Burford Holly)

193   This holly will grow in the hot interior valleys. Bears heavy crops of bright red berries. Self-pollinating. The leaves are smooth, dark green with few spines. Grows to six feet or more, but stands any amount of pruning.   Planting Group 1

195   Kerria japonica

Kalmia latifolia   Zone 4
(Mountain Laurel)

194   Hardy in most all zones, but does not grow too well in California. Slow growing to four or five feet in the west (ten to fifteen feet in the east). Glossy, leathery leaves with clusters of deep pink buds and lighter, one-inch pink flowers. Same culture as Rhododendrons
Planting Group 5

194   Kalmia latifolia

Kerria japonica   Zone 4
195   Deciduous. Open, rounded shrub to six feet with heavily veined bright green foliage and bright yellow flowers from March to May. Likes part shade in warmer areas but will take full sun in cooler coastal areas.   Planting Group 1

Lantana camara   Zone 9

196-197 A popular, rapid-growing shrub that blooms most of the year. Wide range of colors and very easy to grow. Even worthwhile in colder areas, where they freeze, if treated as an annual. It loves hot weather.

Christine   Cerise pink
Orange   Orange
Radiation   Orange red
White   White
Yellow   Yellow

Planting Group 1

197   Lantana camara radiation

196   Lantana camara yellow

198   Leptospermum laevigatum Reevesii

Leptospermum laevigatum Reevesii   Zone 9
(Dwarf Australian Tea Tree)

198 A dwarf form of L. Laevigatum. The leaves are a little more rounded and the shrub grows more compactly. Thrives in the same trying conditions as L. Laevigatum and keeps its nice appearance even with wind, heat, and drought. Good seashore plant to six feet.

Planting Group 1

Leptospermum scoparium 'Helene Strybing'   Zone 9

199 Fine, needle-like foliage, with dark pink, open-faced flowers about one inch in diameter. Some flowers almost the year around with the heavy blooming season in the early spring. Excellent cut flower. Must be planted in a well-drained location.

Planting Group 2

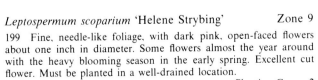

199   Leptospermum scoparium 'Helene Strybing'

200 *Leptospermum scoparium* 'Ruby Glow'

201 *Leucophyllum frutescens*

202 *Ligustrum japonica texanum*

203 *Ligustrum ovalifolium*

Leptospermum scoparium 'Ruby Glow'　　　Zone 9

200 Another of the hybrid Leptospermums that is very fine and certainly has a place in the California garden. The flowers are double red and three-fourths of one inch in diameter. Great masses of blooms in the winter and spring, and in such profusion, the entire shrub turns red. Needs excellent drainage or it will die almost overnight. If it does, try it again in another spot. It is a very worthwhile five to six foot plant.　　　Planting Group 3

Leucophyllum frutescens　　　Zone 8
(Texas Sage or Senisa)

201 Evergreen shrub to about six feet with drought-resistant silver-gray foliage. Will grow near the sea or in the hottest desert. Wants sandy, well-drained soil.　　　Planting Group 3

Ligustrum japonica texanum (L. J. lusterleaf)　　　Zone 8
(Wax Leaf Privet)

202 The leaves are waxy, dark green, spongy, and oval in appearance. Fragrant, wax-white flowers. It also gives off allergy-producing pollen in spring. Will grow higher than six feet, but usually kept at three to five feet.　　　Planting Group 1

Ligustrum ovalifolium　　　Zone 7
(California Privet)

203 The most popular hedge plant in California. Relatively inexpensive and fast growing. Will grow taller than six feet, but is best when kept trimmed to four or five feet. The flowers can cause hay-fever.　　　Planting Group 1

204   *Lippia citriodora*

206   *Mahonia bealei*

Lippia citriodora (Aloysia triphylla)   Zone 8
(Lemon Verbena)

204   A leggy, loose-growing plant to about eight feet that is not much
to look at but a joy to have. It should be placed next to a path where
you can pick a leaf as you go by to rub and smell. Full sun.
                                                        Planting Group 1

Mahonia aquifolium   Zone 5
(Oregon Grape)

205   Native from British Columbia to California. Dwarf, compact
shrub with glossy green, holly-like leaflets, new growth bronzy. Showy
clusters of bright yellow flowers, March to May, followed by blue
berries. Grows in sun or shade. Deer proof.   Planting Group 1

205   *Mahonia aquifolium*

Mahonia bealei   Zone 6
(Siberian Grape)

206   Flat whorls of grayish-green leaves with stiff, spiny teeth on each
leaflet. Excellent for the shade. Very effective against a wall, especially
if lights are used to cast shadows of the leaves. Deer proof.
                                              Planting Group 4

Mahonia lomariifolia   Zone 8
(Chinese Hollygrape)

207   Very large, grayish pinnate leaves up to fifteen inches in length
with each leaflet having deeply-serrated and waxy margins. The flowers are larger and brighter than the American varieties. When young,
grows on a single stalk; later it branches from the base creating an
artistic effect. Recommended for an "Oriental Look" in the garden.
Best in half shade. Can be used indoors in a sunny location with
plenty of room so you can avoid contact with prickly leaves. Usually
a four to six-foot plant, but will grow to ten feet if not cut back.
                                              Planting Group 2

207   *Mahonia lomariifolia*

208   *Mahonia pinnata*

Mahonia pinnata   Zone 7
(California Grape)

208   Similar to Mahonia Aquifolium, but the leaves are more holly-like; has similar long, yellow flowers. Will stand more heat and drought. A very fine, low-growing, decorative shrub. Sun or shade. Deer proof.   Planting Group 1

210   *Michelia fuscata*

211   *Murraya exotica*

209   *Melianthus major*

Melianthus major   Zone 9
(Honey Bush)

209   Large, blue-gray, deeply-toothed foliage one foot long, reddish brown flowers in late winter or early spring. Can grow to six feet in a year and eventually up to eight or nine, and about as wide. Usually too big for the small garden. Needs hand-picking of the old, dry leaves that hang on. Stands any conditions, wet or dry; hot sun or shade.
                          Planting Group 1

Michelia fuscata (M. figo)   Zone 9
(Banana Shrub)

210   A glossy, clean shrub that will eventually grow higher, but best kept under six feet. The flowers are creamy white with brownish backs that lightly perfume the garden with a banana-like fragrance.
                          Planting Group 4

Murraya exotica (M. paniculata)   Zone 9
(Orange Jessamine)

211   Evergreen shrub with luxurious, deep green, small foliage and quantities of small, waxy, white flowers bearing an intense orange-blossom fragrance. Not frost hardy. Likes rich, deep soil; half (or more) shade and regular feeding of high-nitrogen fertilizer, plus iron.   Planting Group 5

212   Myrsine africana

213   Myrtus communis

214   Nandina domestica

215   Nerium oleander 'Single White'

Myrsine africana   Zone 9

(African Box)

212   A four to five-foot shrub similar to boxwood with small rounded dark green leaves. Good in full sun or partial shade and best when kept clipped. Somewhat subject to scale insects.   Planting Group 1

Myrtus communis   Zone 7

(Common Myrtle)

213   One of the oldest shrubs still in cultivation. It dates back to ancient Greece where it was used for Victory wreaths. Rounded shrub to five or six feet with small, pointed leaves that are dark green, glossy and aromatic and an abundance of small, white fluffy flowers.
Planting Group 1

Nandina domestica   Zone 8

(Heavenly Bamboo)

214   Not a bamboo, but the foliage and stems give that impression. Leaves are light green, tipped with red and turn a vivid red in the autumn. White flowers followed by bright red berries. Grows in sun or shade. One of the few outdoor shrubs that can be used indoors in planters if there is enough light. Will grow higher but should be kept thinned out to not more than five or six feet. Planting Group 1

216 *Nerium oleander* 'Single Pink'

217 *Nerium oleander* 'Tree Form Single White'

Nerium oleander   Zone 8
(Oleander)

215-216-217 A wonderful, hot weather shrub. Blooms all summer in the interior valleys, not too well on the coast. Lots of colors; white, rose, red, pink, and all shades in between. Both single and double flowers. The singles are preferred in the garden because the old flowers of the doubles usually hang on and spoil the appearance of the shrub. Will eventually grow taller than a medium-sized shrub, so should be kept pruned to garden size.   Planting Group 1

Osmanthus fragrans   Zone 8
(Sweet Olive)

219 One of the best of the Osmanthus family if kept to a five or six foot shrub. Tiny, fragrant, white flowers are hidden by the foliage on this exceptionally clean-looking shrub. Fragrance in much heavier in the warmer climates. Likes partial shade, but will take full sun on the coast.   Planting Group 1

Osmanthus delavayi   Zone 7

218 Tiny, dark, glossy green foliage. In the spring, this plant is covered with small, white flowers on graceful, arching branches. They have a delightful, spicy fragrance. Wants slightly acid soil and partial shade. Usually a five to six foot shrub but will grow taller if not pruned.   Planting Group 1

218 *Osmanthus delavayi*

219 *Osmanthus fragrans*

220   *Osmanthus ilicifolius*

221   *Osmanthus ilicifolius variegatus*

Osmanthus ilicifolius   Zone 7

(False Holly)

220   A sturdy, erect bush with holly-like foliage that is attractive and clean the year around. Grows to six feet, sometimes taller. Fragrant, small, white flowers in the fall.   Planting Group 4

Osmanthus ilicifolius variegatus   Zone 7

(Variegated False Holly)

221   An evergreen shrub, seldom more than five feet. Dark green, spiny foliage with a creamy white edge. It is much slower growing and much more compact than 0. Ilicifolius. An excellent shrub to break the monotony of a heavy green planting. Best in partial shade and slightly acid conditions.   Planting Group 4

222   *Philadelphus virginalis*

Palms
    All palms are listed together in the Tall shrub section.

Philadelphus virginalis   Zone 4

(Mock Orange)

222   Deciduous. Medium-size shrub to six or eight feet, sometimes taller, bearing quantities of fragrant white flowers in the spring and summer. Stands heavy pruning.   Planting Group 1

Philodendron ‘Evansii’   Zone 9

223   An exotic tropical that does well in partial shade outdoors. Large dark green leaves, two feet wide and as long as four feet. Stout, tree-like trunk with heavy aerial roots that reach the ground. Use indoors or outdoors.   Planting Group 1

223   *Philodendron* ‘Evansii’

224   *Philodendron selloum*

226   *Phormium tenax*

225   *Phormium tenax atropurpureum*

227   *Pieris formosa* 'Forrestii'

Philodendron selloum   Zone 9
(Split Leaf Philodendron)

224   Another lush tropical plant with deeply-lobed elephant-ear leaves up to two feet across. If you have room, plant in clumps, three feet apart for best tropical effect.

Planting Group 1

Phormium tenax   Zone 9
(New Zealand Flax)

225-226   Long, stiff, sword-like leaves. Does as well in the desert as on the coast. A number of varieties are available in the nurseries, some excellent for a tropical or oriental planting. Other varieties: Variegated, bronze, rubra, atropurpurea, etc.   Planting Group 1

Pieris formosa 'Forrestii'   Zone 8
(Chinese Andromeda)

227   More vigorous than P. Japonica. Leaves are longer and wider, and the flowers are three times the size. The most interesting feature of this plant is the brilliant red color of the new foliage. Sometimes the plant will grow taller but is best kept to under eight feet. Same culture as Rhododendrons.   Planting Group 5

231   Pieris japonica 'Variegata'

228   Pieris japonica

Pieris japonica   Zone 5
(Andromeda japonica)
(Lily of the Valley Shrub)

228   An attractive shrub up to six feet with dainty, white, bell-shaped flowers reminding one of a Lily of the Valley. Needs excellent drainage, at least partial or full shade, plenty of peat moss, leaf mold and acid food. Does not like the heat.   Planting Group 5

230   Pieris japonica 'Flamingo Pink'

Pieris japonica 'Flame of the Forest'
                                Zone 6

229   A new cross between P. Forrestii and P. Japonica. Has the many good qualities of the new bright red folidage of P. Forrestii and the white flower clusters and compactness of P. Japonica. Plant in heavy peat moss.
                         Planting Group 5

Pieris japonica 'Flamingo Pink'   Zone 5

230   Same foliage, same size as the popular P. Japonica and needs the same culture. The flowers are a nice shade of pink. Certainly an addition to the garden.   Planting Group 5

Pieris japonica 'Variegata'   Zone 5

231   Very similar to P. Japonica but with striking green leaves edged in white.
                         Planting Group 5

229   Pieris japonica 'Flame of the Forest'

232   Pittosporum tobira

235   Poinciana gilliesii

233   Pittosporum tobira 'Variegata'

Pittosporum tobira   Zone 8
(Japanese Pittosporum)

232   The most widely planted of the Pittosporum family. Will grow higher than six feet, but should be held there or lower by pruning. Foliage dark green and leathery in either sun or shade, flowers are creamy white with a nice fragrance.   Planting Group 2

Pittosporum tobira 'Variegata'   Zone 8

233   Sport of P. Tobira that can easily be held to five feet. The grayish-green foliage is used very effectively in flower arrangements. Prefers a dry location and will grow in either sun or shade.
                                                              Planting Group 2

234   Plumbago capensis

Plumbago capensis   Zone 9
(Cape Plumbago)

234   Half vine, half shrub. Needs support. Left to itself, it will mound up to six feet or more. Foliage is light green and the flowers are masses of pale blue. Needs little care. Full sun. Excellent bank cover.   Planting Group 1

Poinciana gilliesii   Zone 9
(Bird of Paradise Shrub)

235   Shrub or small tree to six or eight feet with light yellow flowers carrying brilliant red stamens and fine feathery foliage. Needs heat, light, and well drained soil.   Planting Group 1

236 *Prunus caroliniana* 'Compacta'

237 *Pyracantha fortuneana* 'Graberi'

Pyracantha fortuneana 'Graberi'　　Zone 7
(Firethorn)

237 Strong-growing shrub with graceful, arching branches, covered with large, bright red berries. One of the best. Of all the broadleaf evergreen shrubs sold, probably the Pyracantha is in the Number 1 spot. Well adapted for espalier. Full sun and plenty of space for this eight to nine-foot plant.　　Planting Group 1

Prunus caroliniana 'Compacta'　Zone 7
(Compact Carolina Cherry)

236 The growth is slower and much more compact than P. Caroliniana making for a very desirable patio shrub.　　Planting Group 1

238 *Raphiolepis ovata*

Raphiolepis ovata (R. umbellata) Zone 7
(Round Leaf Raphiolepis)

238 Round, thick, leathery dark green foliage on a compact, tough shrub to four or five feet. Flowers are white in clusters, followed by blue berries. Sun or shade.　　Planting Group 1

Rhamnus californica　　Zone 8
(California Coffee Berry)

239 A large, spreading shrub that will do well in either sun or shade and grow under very dry conditions. It has long, dark green, glossy foliage. White flowers are followed by green berries that turn red, then black, when ripe. One of the best California natives, but scarce in the trade.　　Planting Group 2

239 *Rhamnus californica*

RHODODENDRONS

Another group of plants that deserve the honor of being called "an Aristocrat of the Garden". From Central California north, especially in the cooler coastal areas, Oregon and Washington, they are at their best. They have a wealth of beautiful, glossy dark green foliage and clusters of gorgeous flowers in the spring.

Rhododendrons are surface feeders and should never be planted any deeper than they were grown in the nursery. In planting, the hole should never be deeper than the ball but should be, especially in heavy soils, at least three feet in diameter. Throw out the heavy soil and make a mixture of peat moss, leaf mold or compost, mixed with a small amount of soil and use this to fill around the plant. None of this fill should be placed underneath the plant, as eventually this medium will rot and allow the plant to settle. (The roots that go down are anchor roots which go after water and are tough enough to penetrate shale.) The roots that make the plant grow are the surface feeder roots; hence, the need for loose soil around the plant. Plants with surface feeder roots do not like to be cultivated as this destroys the growing cycle.

The roots should be shaded from the sun, even in cooler areas; until the plant is big enough to cover the root area it could suffer from sun on the roots.

I have found that a large boulder, (six inches thick and eighteen-inches-plus around,) placed on the sunny side of the plant helps. (If you turn over a rock in a dry field in the summer, it is always damp under the rock.) This method of shading also helps other plants that require moist, shaded roots such as Japanese maples, clematis, camellias, azaleas and others.

Following is a list of a great many of the Rhododendrons now available (but not in all nurseries). Dwarf, medium and tall-growing varieties are listed together in this section as with other families. Some plants will easily grow to twenty feet in one area and only six feet in another.

Rhododendrons should be fed when they finish blooming and may also be cut heavily to shape them at this time. Extremely heavy pruning, say a twenty-foot plant down to four feet, should be done two weeks before the blooming starts.

240B *Rhododendron* 'Vanessa'

240 *Rhododendron* 'Christmas Cheer'

RHODODENDRONS   HARDINESS RATING

A. BEDFORD. Lavender with dark eye. Late May	H3
ALICE. Pink. Early May	H3
ANAH KRUSCHKE. Lavender-blue. June	H3
ANNA ROSE WHITNEY. Deep rose-pink. Late May	H3
ANNIE E. ENDTZ. Bright pink. Early May	H3
ANTOON VAN WELIE. Deep pink. Early May	H3
BETTY WORMALD. Pink with purple blotch. Early May	H3
BLUE BIRD. Blue dwarf. Early April	H3
BLUE DIAMOND. Dwarf, bright blue. Early April	H3
BLUE PETER. Lavender-blue, dark blotch. Early May	H2
BLUE TIT. Dwarf, bright blue. Early April	H3
BOW BELL. Bright pink, semi-dwarf. Early May	H3
BRITANNIA. Red. Late May	H3
BUTTERFLY. Lemon yellow. Early May	H3
CARITA. Pale primrose. Late April	H4
CARRY-ANN. Bright strawberry red. Early May	H3
CHRISTMAS CHEER. Early, light pink. March	H2
CORNUBIA. Large brilliant red. March	H5
COTTON CANDY. Very large flower of pink and white tones. Early May	H3
CUNNINGHAM'S WHITE. White. Late May	H2
CYNTHIA. Deep rose. Late May	H2
DAPHNOIDES. Rosy lilac, dwarf. Late May	H2
DAVID. Blood red. Early May	H4
DONCASTER. Scarlet crimson. Late May	H3
ELIZABETH. Bright red, semi-dwarf. Early April	H3
EUREKA MAID. Deep pink. Early May	H3
EVENING GLOW. Deep yellow. Late May	H3
EVERESTIANUM. Rose lilac. Late May	H2
FORSTERIANUM. Fragrant white. April	H5
FRAGRANTISSIMA. Fragrant white. Early May	H5
GOMER WATERER. Blush fading to white. Late May	H2
GRAF ZEPPELIN. Bright pink. Late May	H3
HARVEST MOON. Lemon yellow. Early May	H3
IMPEDITUM. Purple-blue, dwarf. Early April	H2
JAN DEKENS. Pink, ruffled edge. Early May	H3
JEAN MARIE DE MONTAGUE. Bright scarlet red. Early May	H2
J. H. VAN NES. Soft red. Early May	H3
LADY PRIMROSE. Lemon Yellow	H4
LAMPLIGHTER. Large red. Early May	H3
LAVENDER GIRL. Pale lavender. Early May	H3
LODER'S WHITE. White Early May	H3
LORD ROBERTS. Dark red. June	H2
MARS. Deep true red. Late May	H2
MME. DE BRUIN. Bright red. Late May	H2
MRS. FURNIVAL. Light pink, deep blotch. Early May	H2
MME. MASSON. White with yellow blotch. Late May	H2
MRS. A. T. DE LA MARE. White. Early May	H2
MRS. BETTY ROBERTSON. Large yellow. Early May	H3
MRS. CHARLES PEARSON. Pale blush mauve. Early May	H3

RHODODENDRONS   HARDINESS RATING

MRS. E. C. STIRLING. Blush pink. Early May	H3
MRS. G. W. LEAK. Pink, dark blotch. Early May	H4
OCEAN LAKE. Deep blue dwarf. Early April	H3
ODEE WRIGHT. Yellow. Early	H3
PINK PEARL. Pink. Early May	H3
PURPLE SPLENDOUR. Deep purple, dark blotch. Late May	H2
QUEEN MARY. Large, deep pink. Early May	H2
RAMAPO. Dwarf, violet-blue. Early April	H1
ROYAL PURPLE. Purple, yellow blotch. Late May	H2
SAPPHIRE. Deep blue, dwarf. Early April	H3
SCARLET WONDER. Red. Semi-dwarf. Late April	H2
SAPPHO. White with purple blotch. Early May	H2
SCINTILLATION. Pink. Early May	H2
SOUV. OF W. C. SLOCOCK. Primrose yellow. Early May	H3
TRILBY. Deep crimson, dark blotch. Late May	H2
UNIQUE. Soft lemon. Late April	H3
UNKNOWN WARRIOR. Early bright red. Early April	H3
VULCAN. Bright red. Late May	H2
WILSONAE. Pink, dwarf.	H3

Letters and numbers indicate hardiness rating as follows:

H1 hardy to minus 25°	H4 hardy to plus 5°
H2 hardy to minus 15°	H5 hardy to plus 15°
H3 hardy to minus 5°	

240C   Rhododendron 'Rainbow'

240D   Rhododendron 'Jean Marie de Montague'

240E   Rhododendron 'Sappho'

Did you ever hear of "Blossom Blindness"? Many think it is a good idea to buy Rhododendrons in bloom (and we approve) but many people become so entranced with the bloom, they forget what the plant looks like and, all too often, they go home with a tall, loose-growing variety when they need a compact-growing plant, or vice versa.

240F   Rhododendron 'Mrs. A. Bedford'

240G   Rhododendron 'Purple Splendour'

240H   Rhododendron 'Elizabeth'

240I   Rhododendron 'Mrs. Charles Pearson'

240J   Rhododendron 'Loderi King George'

240K   Rhododendron 'Unknown Warrior'

240M   Rhododendron 'Cilpinense'

240N   Rhododendron 'Rose Elf'

240O   *Rhododendron* 'Ocean Lake'

240L   *Rhododendron* 'Bow Bell'

240P   *Rhododendron* 'Pink Pearl'

240Q   *Rhododendron* 'Mrs. E.C. Sterling'

240R   *Rhododendron* 'Eureka Maid'

240S   *Rhododendron* 'Anna Rose Whitney'

240T   *Rhododendron* 'Mrs. G.W. Leak'

Rhus ovata   Zone 9
(Sugar Bush)

241   Native California evergreen. Usually an erect shrub, five or six
feet tall, and as wide. Nearly round, two to three-inch leaves that
are gray-green, thick, and leathery. The flowers are white or pinkish
in dense clusters. Like its cousin, the poison-oak, (but no rash with
this one), it will stand all conditions; drought in Santa Barbara or
lawn water. Likes sun, poor soil, or good soil. Stands wind or salt
spray. Adaptable to pruning. Really an excellent shrub.
                                      Planting Group 1

241   *Rhus ovata*

242   *Rhus typhina* 'Laciniata'

Rhus typhina 'Laciniata'   Zone 3
(Staghorn Sumac)

242   Deciduous shrub or small tree with divided leaves, dark green
above and grayish underneath turning a rich red in the fall. Stands
extreme heat and cold, garden watering, or drought.
                                      Planting Group 1

243   *Ribes sanguineum*

Ribes sanguineum   Zone 7
(Red Flowering Currant)

243   A very satisfactory, deciduous shrub. Usually grows to six or
eight feet, and is covered in the spring with deep pink to red flowers
having a spicy fragrance.   Planting Group 1.

Romneya coulteri   Zone 7
(Matilija Poppy)

244   One of California's finest natives for a dry hillside. Blooms are
huge, snow-white, "crepe paper" flowers with a large cluster of golden
stamens in the center, reminding one of a fried egg "sunny-side-up".
Has gray-green foliage. Grows to five or six feet, spreads rapidly from
underground roots.   Planting Group 3

244   *Romneya coulteri*

245   Sarcococca ruscifolia

247   Spiraea prunifolia

Sarcococca ruscifolia   Zone 6

245   Medium size shrub to four to five feet tall with equal spread. Dark green foliage with very small and very fragrant white flowers which are followed by small, red berries that later turn black. A shade plant that wants good drainage and only small amounts of water.
                                              Planting Group 5

246   Spartium junceum

248   Spiraea vanhouttei

Spartium junceum   Zone 7
(Yellow Spanish Broom)

246   Excellent plant, both for the seashore and the hot, dry districts. The plants have slender, bright green, almost-leafless, upright branches to eight feet that are covered with fragrant, yellow flowers in the spring.   Planting Group 1

Spiraea prunifolia   Zone 4
(Shoe Button Bridal Wreath)

247   Deciduous. This double-flowered Spiraea grows to about six feet. Upright growth with graceful branches covered in early spring with small, double white flowers along the stem.   Planting Group 1

Spiraea vanhouttei   Zone 4
(Bridal Wreath)

248   Deciduous. In the spring, all'over the country, Spiraea is prized for the tiny, white flowers that entirely clothe the arching branches. The bushes look like they are covered with snow. Planting Group 1

250 *Syringa vulgaris* 'Lavender Lady'

249 *Syringa persica* 'Laciniata'

Syringa persica 'Laciniata'   Zone 5
(Cut Leaf Persian Lilac)

249 Deciduous. Best of the lilacs; adapted to the hot parts of the
west. Fine cut-leaf foliage and lavender flowers. Also grows well in
the cooler coastal regions.   Planting Group 1

251 *Syringa vulgaris* 'Esther Staley'

Syringa vulgaris   Zone 4
(Lilac)

250-251-252-253 Deciduous shrubs. Many named varieties and
various colors; lavender, blue, pink, and white, both double and single
flowers. All are best where winter brings a pronounced chill.They
like an alkaline soil. Where soil is acid, work lime into the soil.
                                               Planting Group 1

252 *Syringa vulgaris* 'Ellen Willmott'

253 *Syringa vulgaris* 'Vulcan'

254   Ternstroemia japonica

255   Teucrium fruticans

256   Vaccinum ovatum

Ternstroemia japonica   Zone 7

254   One of the finest landscape shrubs in the trade. Grows compactly to five or six feet (sometimes taller) and as broad. Handsome, dark green, camellia-like foliage has a bronzy cast in the shade and a much bronzier cast in the sun, turning to red in the fall and winter. A relative of the Camellia, so give it the same soil culture.   Planting Group 4

257   Viburnum suspensum

Teucrium fruticans   Zone 8
(Germander)

255   Light gray foliage and pale blue flowers almost the year around. It requires a hot, dry, well-drained soil.   Planting Group 3

Vaccinum ovatum   Zone 8
(Evergreen Huckleberry)

256   Native to hills close to the coast, from Monterey north to British Columbia. Erect plant with leathery, dark green foliage. Pinkish flowers in the spring, followed by berries that are blue-black and excellent for pies and jam. Best in partial shade. Cut branches popular with florists.   Planting Group 2.

Viburnum suspensum   Zone 8
(Sandankwa Viburnum)

257   A handsome, dense shrub with glossy green, wrinkled leaves. Use as a specimen or hedge, as it is neat and attractive at all times. Sun or shade.   Planting Group 1

Weigela florida 'Bristol Ruby'   Zone 5

258   Deciduous. Well known shrub producing masses of red flowers in the spring and summer. Prune after flowering to develop new wood for next year's flowers. Sun. Grows anywhere.   Planting Group 1

258   Weigela florida 'Bristol Ruby'

Weigela florida 'Rosea'   Zone 5

(Pink Weigela)

259   Deciduous. Large clusters of bright pink flowers in spring and early summer. This is the common pink variety well known all over the United States. Grows anywhere but does best in full sun and should be pruned heavily after blooming. Will grow to ten feet, but should be pruned down to five in July, then allowed to grow.
                                                           Planting Group 1

259   Weigela florida 'Rosea'

Xylosma senticosa (X. congestum)   Zone 8

(Shiny Xylosma)

260   Here is an excellent shrub for any place in the garden, tough or not. Takes a hot location or part shade. Excellent trained on the wall as an espalier. The foliage is light yellow apple green color. Will grow much taller than six feet, but best kept pruned to this height.
                                                           Planting Group 1

260   Xylosma senticosa

TALL GROWING SHRUBS

Plants in this group usually grow to nine feet or more. All are
evergreen unless otherwise mentioned.

261   *Aralia papyrifera*

Aralia papyrifera   Zone 8
(Rice Paper Plant)

261   Plant this for a tropical effect. It is tall and bold with greenish-
gray leaves, often fifteen inches across. It is difficult to grow anything
underneath this plant.   Planting Group 3

262   *Arbutus unedo*

Arbutus unedo   Zone 8
(Strawberry Tree)

262   The dark green foliage resembles the native California Toyon.
When mature, the tree produces clusters of small, bell-shaped flowers,
which develop into bright red "strawberries". Deer proof.
                                                 Planting Group 3

Azara microphylla   Zone 8
(Box Leaf Azara)

263   Tall growing shrub or small tree with tiny boxwood-like foliage.
Fan-like branching makes it ideal to spread out against a high, blank
wall. Sun or partial shade.   Planting Group 1

263   *Azara microphylla*

266   *Bambusa phyllostachys* 'Nigra'

264   *Bambusa phyllostachys* 'Aurea'

Bambusa phyllostachys 'Aurea'   Zone 8
(Golden Bamboo)

264   This is the most popular variety of Bamboo. It grows to approximately fifteen feet. Sun or shade. Good tub plant. The cost of bamboo is usually almost double that of other plants, because nurserymen cannot propagate it in the usual way. It must be grown, divided, then established again, making a double process of growing. Invasive, unless roots are restricted   Planting Group 1

Bambusa phyllostachys 'Bambusoides'   Zone 8
(Giant Timber Bamboo)

265   The poles are up to four inches in diameter and will grow to a height of thirty to forty feet if given plenty of heat and water.
                    Planting Group 1

Bambusa phyllostachys 'Nigra'   Zone 8
(Black Bamboo)

266   Grows to about ten feet, with the poles turning black. Great favorite in an Oriental planting.   Planting Group 1

Beaucarnea recurvata   Zone 9
(Bottle Ponytail)

267   Native to the dry regions of Texas and Mexico. Likes a dry exposed spot with rich, well-drained sandy loam. Will stand dry desert conditions. It is a Dracaena-like plant with a tall trunk and swollen base. Excellent tub plant.   Planting Group 3

265   *Bambusa phyllostachys* 'Bambusoides'

267   *Beaucarnea recurvata*

268   *Callistemon lanceolatus*

270   *Carpenteria californica*

Callistemon lanceolatus   Zone 9
(Lemon Bottlebrush)

268   Rounded shrub or small tree to fifteen feet. Flowers look like bunches of bright red brushes in May and June, and again later in the season. Very showy; stands sun and drought. Also trained as a tree.   Planting Group 1

Ceanothus arboreus 'Ray Hartman'
                                              Zone 8

271   One of the new hybrid varieties of Ceanothus. A small tree (to fifteen feet) that can be maintained as a large shrub with some pruning. Large, dark green leaves and bright blue flowers three to five inches long, borne in open clusters.   Planting Group 2

Callistemon viminalis   Zone 9
(Weeping Bottlebrush)

269   When used as a specimen, it makes a dense mass of brilliant fire-red bottlebrushes. Grows to fifteen feet and stands sun; does not like wind or a very dry area. Also trained as a tree.
                                              Planting Group 1

Carpenteria californica   Zone 8
(Bush Anemone)

270   One of the finest California Natives. Thick, dark green foliage that is white underneath. From June to August has white two-inch anemone-like flowers. One of the natives that will take garden watering in the summer if it has good drainage. Very scarce.
                                              Planting Group 2

271   *Ceanothus arboreus*, 'Ray Hartman'

269   *Callistemon viminalis*

272   *Ceanothus cyaneus,* 'Sierra Blue'

275   *Cocculus laurifolius*

Ceanothus cyaneus, 'Sierra Blue'   Zone 8

272   Vigorous, large-growing shrub with dark green foliage and large plume flowers of bright blue in spring. Grows to about ten feet, but can be kept pruned.   Planting Group 2

Cercis canadensis   Zone 4
(Eastern Redbud)

273   Deciduous. Medium-sized, round-headed tree or shrub. Small, rose-pink flowers clothe bare, brown branches in early spring.
                                                         Planting Group 1

273   *Cercis canadensis*

Cercis occidentalis   Zone 5
(Western Red Bud)

274   Deciduous. Bush or small tree covered with magenta, sweet-pea-shaped flowers, followed by handsome three-inch diameter leaves. In the fall, it has "Autumn" color.   Planting Group 2

Cocculus laurifolius   Zone 8
(Laurelleaf Snailseed)

275   Excellent background shrub in the shade or sun. Will grow to ten feet or more with graceful arching foliage of a beautiful dark green. Leaves are four to five inches long. Stands heavy pruning. Tolerates poor soil. Foliage good for flower arrangements. It is not used enough.   Planting Group 1 or 4

274   *Cercis occidentalis*

276   Cortaderia selloana

277   Cotinus coggygria

Cortaderia selloana (C. argentea)   Zone 5

(Pampas Grass)

276   Giant ornamental grass. Very conspicuous plume flowers in pink or white that grow half again as tall as the plant. Grows in any soil and becomes a pest, as large clumps are almost impossible to dig out by hand. Not for the small garden. Fast growing, dry location.
Planting Group 1

Cotinus Coggygria (Rhus cotinus)   Zone 3

(Smoke tree)

277-278   A tall bush to about nine feet and about as wide as it is tall. Grows best when under stress in poor or rocky soil. Seldom good in a highly cultivated garden. Foliage bluish-green with large clusters of fuzzy purple hairs. Variety Purpureus, which is also shown here, has purple foliage throughout the summer. Both deciduous.
Planting Goup 3

278   Cotinus coggygria 'Purpureus'

Cotoneaster franchetii   Zone 5

279   Fountain-like arching growth to ten feet or more and as wide; however, in poor soil without summer water, only to five or six feet. Small, pinkish flowers followed by orange-red berries borne in clusters.
Planting Group 1

Cotoneaster pannosa   Zone 7

(Silverleaf Cotoneaster)

280   Tall, graceful shrub with gray foliage and long arching branches. White flowers followed by bright red berries. Can be used as a quick-growing tall background or a screen shrub. It requires little attention or water and will stand unlimited pruning.
Planting Group 1

279   Cotoneaster franchetii

280   Cotoneaster pannosa

281   *Cotoneaster parneyi*

284   *Dodonaea viscosa* 'Purpurea'

282   *Cyperus papyrus*

283   *Datura suaveolens*

Cotoneaster parneyi   Zone 8
(Red Cluster Berry)

281   One of the best of the upright Cotoneasters with graceful, arching branches. It spreads wider, (eight feet), than it grows tall. Thick, dark green foliage with heavy clusters of red berries that hang on most of the winter.   Planting Group 1

Cyperus papyrus   Zone 9
(Egyptian Paper Reed)

282   Tall, reed-like stems to eight feet, topped by an eight-inch umble of lacy, thread-like grass. Plant in a wet spot; it is one of the few plants that can be planted in a fish pond. Very effective in an Oriental or Tropical planting. Sun or shade.   Planting Group 1

Datura suaveolens   Zone 9
(Angel's Trumpet)

283   Fast-growing evergreen shrub, sometimes a small tree to eight or ten feet. Large, ten   inch long leaves and lots of large, white bell-shaped flowers about eight inches long and four inches wide at the bottom, which continue to appear all summer. Planting Group 1

Dodonaea viscosa 'Purpurea'   Zone 9
(Purple Leaf Dodonaea or Hopseed Bush)

284   A fast-growing shrub or small tree from New Zealand. Excellent landscape effect is obtained when used as a tall screen and is kept thinned. It turns brilliant purple as soon as cold weather hits it. In the spring, it turns back to its natural rusty green. Different. Very interesting.   Planting Group 1

285   *Dracaena indivisa*

286   *Elaeagnus pungens*

287   *Elaeagnus pungens* 'Maculata'

288   *Escallonia fradesii*

Dracaena indivisa   Zone 8
(Cordyline indivisa)

(Dracaena Palm)

285   A tall plant associated with Spanish architecture, but native to New Zealand. Grows to fifteen feet and makes a striking effect with its narrow lance-like leaves that grow as "top-nots" on a thick, gray trunk. Plant singly or in clumps.   Planting Group 1

Elaeagnus pungens   Zone 6

(Silver Berry)

286   Wavy, gray-green leaves above and silver and brownish underneath. Grows without care to ten feet. Stands drought.
                                        Planting Group 1

Elaeagnus pungens 'Maculata'   Zone 6
287   Much more popular than E. Pungens. The foliage is beautifully marked in gold. A fine spreading plant that will stand drought, heavy pruning, and can be trained along a fence as an espalier.
                                        Planting Group 1

Escallonia 'Fradesii'   Zone 7
288   Medium to tall-growing shrub to ten feet, with a very compact, branching habit. Showy rose-pink flowers in clusters from spring through summer.   Planting Group 1.

289   *Escallonia montevidensis*

291   *Eugenia myrtifolia*

290   *Escallonia organensis*

292   *Feijoa sellowiana*

Escallonia montevidensis   Zone 7
(White Escallonia)

289   The tallest grower of the Escallonia group, often fifteen to twenty feet. The foliage is glossy green, the flower panicles are white. Stands extreme pruning. Excellent on the coast.   Planting Group 1

Escallonia organensis   Zone 7
(Pink Escallonia)

290   Excellent tall shrub for background and screening. Flowers in large clusters of delicate pink to white. Not too good in salt spray areas as the tips will burn.   Planting Group 1

Eugenia myrtifolia (Syzigium paniculata)   Zone 9
(Brush Cherry)

291   Much used in light, front areas as an accent specimen. Usually trimmed to a pyramidal shape. The new foliage is bronzy-red. Small white flowers followed by three-quarter-inch berries of dark lavender. Extensively used for hedges and will make a nice tree to twenty-five feet if allowed to go untrimmed. Will tip burn at about twenty-eight degrees.   Planting Group 1

FERNS

All ferns, regardless of height are listed together in medium shrub section.

Feijoa sellowiana   Zone 8
(Pineapple Guava)

292   One of the best of the flowering and fruiting shrubs. This gray-foliage plant will grow to ten feet, but can be easily kept at six or seven feet. Flowers are white with bright red stamens, followed by edible fruit of a very delicate flavor.   Planting Group 2

293   *Ficus benjamina*

294   *Ficus elastica* 'Decora'

Ficus benjamina   Zone 10
(Weeping Fig)

293   Outstanding small evergreen tree or large shrub with rich shiny green foliage of weeping habit. Used outdoors in the warmer areas of California and indoors elsewhere.   Planting Group 3

295   *Ficus retusa nitida*

Ficus elastica 'Decora'   Zone 9
(Rubber Tree)

294   Small tree or large shrub. One of the most popular indoor plants available; used outside in warm climates.   Planting Group 1

Ficus retusa nitida   Zone 9
(Indian Laurel)

295   Thick leathery rich green leaves on this handsome evergreen. Grown as a trimmed pyramid, a rounded patio tree, a globe and many other ways.   Planting Group 1

Fremontia californica   Zone 9
(Flannel Bush)

296   A small California native tree or large shrub to twelve feet requiring a dry location. Showy, large yellow flowers are born profusely in spring and summer. If watered in the summer, it will grow vigorously for a year or so and then die.   Planting Group 3

296   *Fremontia californica*

299   *Hakea suaveolens*

Griselinia littoralis   Zone 9
(Kupuka Tree)

298   A tree in New Zealand and here a shrub to over ten feet, but
we like it best when kept pruned to about six feet. Use as a compact
hedge or windbreak. Will grow along the ocean, with or without water,
but does best with water. Has dense, rich green handsome foliage.
Not too good in the hot interior.   Planting Group 1

Hakea suaveolens   Zone 9

299   Shrub or small tree to ten or fifteen feet. The foliage is stiff,
needle-like, and bright shiny green, even under drought conditions.
Excellent on the seashore.   Planting Group 2

Hydrangea paniculata grandiflora, 'Peegee'   Zone 4
(Peegee Hydrangea)

300   Deciduous shrub or small tree to ten or fifteen feet. Leaves five
to six inches long turn bronzy in the fall. Large showy flowers in
clusters about a foot long open white; then as they age, fade to pinkish
bronze.   Planting Group 7

297   *Grewia caffra*

Grewia caffra   Zone 9

297   Fast-growing shrub to eight or ten feet
with a rather sprawling habit. A natural espalier. Easy to control. Prune often. The flowers
are prolific, dainty lavender with yellow centers,
from late spring to fall.   Planting Group 2

298   *Griselinia littoralis*

300   *Hydrangea paniculata grandiflora*, 'Peegee'

301   *Ilex altaclarensis* 'Wilsonii'

302   *Ilex aquifolium*

Ilex altaclarensis 'Wilsonii'   Zone 6

301   A bold, decorative shrub or small tree with large thick shiny green leaves and bright red berries. This holly is self-fertile. Makes a good hedge or screen in both sun and shade.   Planting Group 1

Ilex aquifolium   Zone 6
(English Holly)

302   The traditional holly of Christmas. A tall shrub or small tree to twenty feet with glossy green spiny foliage, and red berries borne on female plants. Unfortunately, holly berries are a sad subject for most nurserymen who neglect to tell their customers a male plant is needed for berries. Most hollys are subject to scale insects so should be sprayed regularly. All will stand unlimited pruning.   Planting Group 1

Ilex aquifolium 'Variegata'   Zone 6

303   Golden variegated form of English Holly. Green spiny leaves with a gold edge. Very striking. Male and female plants required to produce berries.   Planting Group 1

Kolkwitzia amabilis   Zone 6
(Beauty Bush)

304   Deciduous. A beautiful ten to twelve-foot bush with graceful arching branches and clusters of small, pink, trumpet-like flowers in May and June. Stands pruning. Likes sun but will stand some shade.   Planting Group 1

303   *Ilex aquifolium* 'Variegata'

304   *Kolkwitzia amabilis*

306   Lagunaria pattersonii

305   Lagerstroemia indica

Larunaria pattersonii   Zone 9
(Sugar Plum Tree)

306   A fast-growing tree or large shrub with a columnar habit. Two-inch pink hibiscus-like flowers that have an interesting seed pod prized by flower arrangers. Excellent at the seashore.
                                          Planting Group 1

Lagerstroemia indica   Zone 7
(Crape Myrtle)

305   Deciduous. Large shrub or small tree grown for its beautiful summer flowers. Colors are white, pink, lavender and rose. Not good on the coast where it mildews, or in the shade in the interior. When planted in a warm spot it is worth a space in any garden. Varieties:

L.I. Alba	White
L.I. Purpurea	Lavender
L.I. Rosea	Pink
L.I. Rubra	Dark rose red
L.I. Watermelon	Rosy red

                          Planting Group 1

Laurus nobilis   Zone 9
(Grecian Laurel)

307   Wonderful compact-growing evergreen shrub. The leaves are the "bay" leaves used in cooking. Often grown as a standard or globe.
                                          Planting Group 2

307   Laurus nobilis

309   Leptospermum scoparium 'Keatleyii'

308   Leptospermum laevigatum

Leptospermum laevigatum   Zone 9

(Australian Tea)

308 Small tree with small, gray-green foliage and white flowers. Excellent as a screen, or windbreak. Will grow and thrive under very trying conditions, even at the ocean's edge. Old specimens twist into interesting shapes with gnarled trunks.   Planting Group 2

Leptospermum scoparium 'Keatleyii'   Zone 9

(Tea Tree)

309 One of the finest of the new group of Leptospermum Hybrids. Will grow to ten feet, but readily kept at six feet. The foliage is rather needle-like with large, open-faced single pink flowers from December to April. Cut flowers are excellent in an arrangement. Wants a well-drained sunny location.   Planting Group 2

Leucadendron argenteum   Zone 10

(Silver Tree)

310 Large evergreen shrub or tree to fifteen feet with silky, silvery white leaves that densely cover irregularly shaped branches. It needs fast-draining soil, will not grow in clay nor alkaline soil and it will not stand animal manure. Very scarce in the trade.
                                               Planting Group 3

310   Leucadendron argenteum

311A   Magnolia 'Campbellii'

311B   Magnolia 'Denudata'

MAGNOLIAS

Oriental magnolia   Zone 6

(Deciduous Tulip Trees)

311   The Magnolias as a group, together with two or three other groups of plants, have often been called the "aristocrats of the garden." There are about a dozen varieties generally in the trade and all are somewhat fragrant. Any of them are worthy of the most favored spot in the garden. They like sun and well-drained peaty soil, with plenty of summer water. They do not like drying winds in the summer or surface cultivation. All will make a tree in about twenty years. A few of the most widely-distributed varieties are:

Magnolia 'Campbelli'

311A   Huge pink flowers up to twelve inches. Many years before this variety will bloom.

Magnolia denudata (M. conspicua)
(Yulan magnolia)
311B   Large pure white flower.

Magnolia liliflora 'Nigra'
311C   Dark purple flowers. A pointed, cup-shaped flower is pink on the inside.

Magnolia soulangiana
(Saucer magnolia)
311D   An attractive, large shrub or small tree that produces a very showy lavendar-pink and white flower before the leaves appear.

Magnolia soulangiana 'Lennei'
311E   Saucer-shaped blooms, eight inches across. Flowers outside are purple rose, inside nearly white. Fragrant.

Magnolia soulangiana 'Grace Me Dade'
311F   Flowers very large; up to ten inches across with deep purplish-pink outside and white inside.

Magnolia soulangiana 'Alexandrina'
311G   Large, tulip-shaped blooms, white inside, purplish-pink outside. A vigorous grower with large rich green foliage.

Magnolia soulangiana 'Lennei Alba'
311H   Vigorous growing with a large globe-shaped creamy white flower.

Magnolia soulangiana 'Rustica Rubra'
311I   Deepest purple of all. White inside.

Magnolia 'Stellata' *(Star magnolia)*
311J   The flowers are composed of many narrow petals, three to four inches across. White.

ALL PLANTING GROUP 1

311C   Magnolia liliflora 'Nigra'

311D   Magnolia soulangiana

311E   Magnolia soulangiana 'Lennei'

311F   Magnolia soulangiana 'Grace Mc Dade'

311G   Magnolia soulangiana 'Alexandrina'

311H   Magnolia soulangiana 'Lennei Alba'

311I   Magnolia soulangiana 'Rustica Rubra'

311J   Magnolia 'Stellata'

311K   Magnolia 'Denudata'

313   *Musa ensete*

312   *Melaleuca decussata*

Melaleuca decussata   Zone 9
(Lilac Melaleuca)

312   Large shrub which stands the windswept conditions of the California coast. Tiny half inch long leaves on arching, pendulous branches and pinkish lavender flowers in abundance from May to September.
                                                  Planting Group 1

Myoporum laetum   Zone 9

315   Very large evergreen shrub or small tree. Fast growing to six feet or more the first year, later to twenty-five or thirty feet. Dense foliage or small, one-by-three-inch, dark, shiny green leaves. Very resistant to salt air and one of the fastest growing oceanside windbreaks. Not good except along the coast. Can be heavily pruned. Also trained as a tree.
                              Planting Group 1

Musa ensete (Ensete ventricosum)   Zone 9
(Banana Tree)

313   Here is tropical atmosphere at its best. Huge long leaves (up to eight feet long and fifteen inches wide) with a heavy red or brownish midrib. Must be protected from strong winds which will shred the leaves; best planted against a tall wall or building. If you want it to grow fast, plant it with a full sack of steer manure in a large hole and keep it wet.
                                                  Planting Group 1

Musa maurelii (Ensete maurelii)   Zone 9
(Red Leaf Banana or Ethiopian Banana)

314   Huge broad tropical foliage. Leaves are wine-red underneath as well as on top. Fast growing but must be protected from wind, as well as cold, as it tears easily.
                                                  Planting Group 1

315   *Myoporum laetum*

314   *Musa maurelii*

Osmanthus fortunei   Zone 7

316 A hybrid between O. fragrans and O. ilicifolius. Fairly slow, bushy growth to seven to ten feet. Leaves are spiny, ovate and dark green. Excellent shrub in the shade, but will take full sun in the cooler regions on the coast. Likes leaf mold and slightly acid conditions.

Planting Group 1

316 *Osmanthus fortunei*

PALMS

All palms, regardless of height, are listed together.

Chamaerops excelsa (Trachycarpus fortunei)   Zone 8
(Windmill Palm)

317 Very handsome palm. Trunk densely covered with black, hairy fibers. The crown is compact and the small, slender fan palm leaves form a thick mat.   Planting Group 1

Chamaerops humilis   Zone 8
(Mediterranean Fan Palm)

318 A multi-trunk fan palm forming a compact green crown on each trunk. Very slow grower.   Planting Group 1

318 *Chamaerops humilis*

317 *Chamaerops excelsa*

319   *Cocos australis*

320   *Cocos plumosa*

Cocos australis (Butia capitata)   Zone 8
(Hardy Blue Cocos)

319   Stands more heat, frost and drought exposure than any of the feather palms. Graceful silver-blue recurved leaf fronds. Retains its bushy form for many years and is an excellent tub plant for a hot sunny exposure.   Planting Group 1

Cocos plumosa (Arecastrum romanzoffianum)   Zone 9
(Queen Palm)

320   Upright growth to thirty feet with long, graceful fronds. Rapid growing and does well in a landscape with other plants. It is used singly or in groups.   Planting Group 1

321   *Cycas revoluta*

Cycas revoluta   Zone 8
(Sago Palm)

321   Extremely slow growing, fern-like in appearance. Usually considered a full sun plant but best with part shade. Attractive pot plant but do not over-water. Not a true palm, but a primitive plant that bears cones and is related to the conifers.   Planting Group 1

322   *Erythea armata*

Erythea armata   Zone 8
(Mexican Blue Palm)

322   A tall palm with a fine spreading crown of rich silver-blue fan-like fronds. Slow growing.   Planting Group 1

324   Phoenix canariensis

Erythea edulis   Zone 9
(Guadalupe Fan Palm)

323   The best fan palm. The large fan-shaped fronds stay bright and fresh summer and winter. The spent fronds fall, naturally cleaning the trunk.   Planting Group 1

Phoenix canariensis   Zone 8
(Canary Island Date Palm)

324   A fast growing palm to fifty feet that forms an immense crown of dark green graceful fronds. Too large for any but the big garden.   Planting Group 1

Phoenix reclinata   Zone 8
(Senegal Date Palm)

325   Probably the most picturesque palm of all, especially when grown in a clump. The fronds are long and graceful.   Planting Group 1

323   Erythea edulis

Phoenix roebelenii   Zone 10
(Pygmy Date Palm)

326   A fine-leafed small-scale palm. Outdoors only in the warmer areas but a house plant everywhere else. A slow grower to a ten-foot stem with cruved, fern-like leaves on a dense crown. Needs moisture and good light indoors.   Planting Group 3

325   Phoenix reclinata

326   Phoenix roebelenii

328   Seaforthia elegans

327   Rhapis excelsa

Rhapis excelsa   Zone 9
(Lady Palm)

327   One of the finest container palms but resents poor light, dust
and drought. Outdoors (it's hardy to twenty degrees) it is best in the
shade.   Planting Group 5

Washingtonia filifera   Zone 8
(California Fan Palm)

329   Native of California. Large four to five-foot broad fan-shaped
leaves on this fast-growing, drought-resistant palm. It grows to fifty
feet or more.   Planting Group 1

Seaforthia elegans   Zone 9
(*Archontophoenix cunninghamiana*)
(King Palm)

328   Tall, slender trunk with long arching
bright green fronds.   Planting Group 1

Washingtonia robusta   Zone 8
(Mexican Fan Palm)

330   Tall, slender trunk, commonly swollen at the base, with brilliant
green fan-shaped fronds. Picturesque in appearance
                                                      Planting Group 1

329   Washingtonia filifera

330   Washingtonia robusta

Photinia arbutifolia (Heteromeles arbutifolia)   Zone 8
(California Toyon)

331 California's most beautiful native shrub during the Holiday
Season with its profusion of red berries. Takes garden conditions,
although sometimes hard to establish. Very young one-gallon-size
plants are best to start. Try to pick a spot where there is perfect drainage.   Planting Group 3

Photinia 'Fraseri'   Zone 8
332 A very interesting, highly ornamental, fast-growing vigorous
shrub. Bright red stems and brilliant red juvenile leaves. Mature foliage
dark green. Clusters of white flowers in spring. Mildew resistant. Also
trained as a tree.   Planting Group 1

Photinia serrulata   Zone 8
(Chinese Photinia)

333 Large shrub or small tree to twenty feet if not controlled by
pruning. This shrub has a lot of good points and some bad. It has
handsome, green four to seven-inch leaves that are bronze when they
first come out. In the fall the two-year-old leaves turn a fire-engine
red and stay on all winter. In April, the plant is covered with five
to seven-inch clusters of small white flowers followed by small red
berries in the winter. The bad points are aphids and mildew. A regular
spray program is necessary. Grows in full sun. Best in the interior.   Planting Group 1

Pittosporum crassifolium   Zone 9
(Karo Pittosporum)

334 One of the fastest growing of all the Pittosporums. Grows very
rapidly to ten feet; then, eventually to twenty-five feet. Gray foliage,
one-half inch by two inches, and maroon flowers in clusters. Drought
resistant. Takes seashore conditions. Stands heavy pruning.   Planting Group 1

331 *Photinia arbutifolia*

332 *Photinia* 'Fraseri'

334 *Pittosporum crassifolium*

333 *Photinia serrulata*

335   *Pittosporum eugenioides*

337   *Pittosporum rhombifolium*

Pittosporum phillyraeoides   Zone 9
(Desert Willow)

336   Large shrub or small weeping tree to fifteen feet that takes poor soil and extreme heat. Fragrant yellow flowers in the spring.
                                                          Planting Group 1

Pittosporum eugenioides   Zone 9
(Tarata Pittosporum)

335   Erect growth. Tall, bushy plant with long, narrow, wavy yellowish-green foliage. Excellent hedge plant or for screen to fifteen or twenty feet. Any soil. Stands drought.
                        Planting Group 1

Pittosporum rhombifolium   Zone 9
(Diamond Leaf Pittosporum)

337   Another large shrub or small tree with diamond-shaped light green leaves, white flowers followed by orange and black berries. Best where there are mild winters.   Planting Group 1

336   *Pittosporum phillyraeoides*

338   *Pittosporum tenuifolium*

339   *Pittosporum undulatum*

Pittosporum tenuifolium (P. nigricans)   Zone 8

(Black Stem Pittosporum)

338   Small two inch light green foliage, used as a screen plant or excellent as a hedge plant. The best plant for a trimmed, pyramidal shape to take the place of Eugenia in the colder climates.
Planting Group 1

Pittosporum undulatum   Zone 9

(Victorian Box)

339   Beautiful, large shrub or round-headed tree to forty feet in the warmer areas. Rich luxuriant, dark green foliage imparts a tropical effect. Very fragrant, creamy white flowers in the spring.
Planting Group 1

Pleroma grandiflora   Zone 9
(*Tibouchina semidecandra*)

(Princess Flower)

340   Velvety leaves and large (two or three-inch) purple flowers borne in profusion all over the plant; which grows about eight to ten feet tall and as wide. For weeks, the ground underneath this plant is purple with the flower petals as they fall to the ground. One of the showiest of the subtropicals with rapid, somewhat leggy, growth habit. Stands heavy pruning in early spring. It is worthwhile to plant in May as an annual in colder areas.
Planting Group 1

341   *Podocarpus elongatus* 'Gracilior'

Podocarpus 'Gracilior' *(P. elongatus)*   Zone 9
(Fern Pine)

341   Actually a conifer. Soft pendulous branches make this plant a delight to any landscape plan. Can be grown in the coastal sun, full shade, or in a pot indoors, and it is excellent as an espalier. Also trained as a tree.
Planting Group 2 or 5

Podocarpus macrophyllus   Zone 9
(Yew Pine)

342   Slower growing than P. Elongatus with broader and longer, dark green leaves. Usually grown as a formal pyramid plant to ten feet. Stands hedge shearing type of pruning. Excellent tub plant, either in the sun or shade.
Planting Group 2

340   *Pleroma grandiflora*

342   *Podocarpus macrophyllus*

343   *Podocarpus macrophyllus* 'Maki'

Podocarpus macrophyllus 'Maki' Zone 9

343   This shrub has black-green leaves, smaller and more rigid than P. Macrophyllus. It is evergreen and will grow inside or in full sun.
Planting Group 2 or 5

347   *Prunus laurocerasus*

Prunus caroliniana   Zone 8
(Carolina Cherry)

344   Large shrub or small tree ideal for screen planting or specimen shrub. Glossy, light green foliage and small white flowers followed by black cherries.   Planting Group 1

Prunus ilicifolia   Zone 8
(Holly Leaf Cherry)

345   Tall shrub with holly-like leaves useful for background planting or a screening. Wants dry, well-drained soil and full sun.
Planting Group 2

Prunus 'Lyonii' *(P. integrifolia)*   Zone 8
(Catalina Cherry)

346   Leaves are as glossy as Prunus Ilicifolia, but double the size (about four or five inches long) and fairly smooth. Excellent tall hedge plant in dry areas. Prefers sun, but will take some shade. Will stand very heavy pruning.   Planting Group 1

344   *Prunus caroliniana*

345   *Prunus ilicifolia*

346   Prunus 'Lyonii'

348   Prunus lusitanica

Prunus laurocerasus   Zone 7

(English Laurel)

347   Fast-growing shrub or small tree to twenty feet, if not pruned. Grown as a foundation shrub, if kept to six or eight feet. The leaves are thick and leathery and always have a fresh green look. Sun or shade.   Planting Group 1

Prunus lusitanica   Zone 7

(Portugal Laurel)

348   Slower growing than English Laurel and the leaves are much smaller. Makes a dense shrub, usually not over eight feet or so, but can become much larger. Stands unlimited pruning. Any soil. Sun or shade.   Planting Group 1

Psidium cattleianum   Zone 10

(Red Strawberry Guava)

349   Large, evergreen, glossy-leaved shrub that bears edible, straw-berry-flavored fruit. Very good for jelly.   Planting Group 1

Punica granatum   Zone 7

(Pomegranate)

350   Deciduous tree or large shrub. Showy, orange-red flowers, some varieties producing pomegranates. Narrow, glossy, bright green leaves. Best in the warmest areas.
Planting Group 1

349   Psidium catteianum

350   Punica granatum

351   Pyracantha coccinea 'Lalandi'

353   Rhamnus alaternus 'Variegata'

Rhamnus alaternus   Zone 7
(Italian Buckthorn)

352   Excellent, fast-growing, clean-looking shrub for either sun or shade. Tolerant to heat, drought or wind. Grows to twenty feet but stands pruning so it can be kept tall and narrow.   Planting Group 1

Pyracantha coccinea 'Lalandi'   Zone 7
351   Tall growing with orange berries. This variety will stand much more cold weather and the branches are very stiff and upright.
                                    Planting Group 1

Rhamnus alaternus 'Variegata'   Zone 7
353   This one does not grow quite as tall or fast as R. Alaternus but can easily grow to ten feet and like its parent, takes drought or garden watering, heat or wind, full sun or part shade. Keep the occasional green stems that show cut out.   Planting Group 1

Rhus integrifolia   Zone 9
(Lemonade Berry)

354   Evergreen. Leathery, nearly round leaves (to about two inches) on a shrub to ten feet or more. Pinkish-white flowers followed by flat, sticky, dark-red fruit. A fine shrub.   Planting Group 2

352   Rhamnus alaternus

354   Rhus integrifolia

355   Stranvaesia davidiana

356   Strelitzia nicolai

Stranvaesia davidiana   Zone 7

355   A wide-spreading shrub to about fifteen feet that is best if given plenty of room in the sun. White flowers in June followed by red berries and bronze foliage suitable for holiday cutting. Best in the Northwest.   Planting Group 1

Strelitzia nicolai   Zone 9

(Giant Bird of Paradise)

356   Tall, tree-like growth with large banana-like leaves and large, bird-like blue and white flowers in fall and winter. Excellent tropical accent plant.   Planting Group 1

Tamarix tetrandra   Zone 6
(Tamarisk)

357   Large, graceful shrub to fifteen feet in height and fifteen to twenty feet across with two-inch-long, pink flowers in clusters.
                                        Planting Group 1

Tecoma capensis (Tecomaria capensis)   Zone 9

(Cape Honeysuckle)

358   This large evergreen shrub or vine is mentioned also in the vine section. It is used as often as a mounded shrub as it is a vine. Dark green, evergreen foliage with bright chinese-red clusters of trumpet-shaped flowers. Excellent at the seashore but it needs good drainage.   Planting Group 3

358   Tecoma capensis

357   Tamarix tetrandra

360   Viburnum burkwoodii

359   Tupidanthus calyptratus

361   Viburnum japonicum

362   Viburnum macrocephalum 'Sterile'

Tupidanthus calyptratus   Zone 10

359   A valuable, exotic, landscape plant in the warmer areas where it may be grown outdoors. This is a tall-growing plant with schefflera-like leaves and an excellent large tub plant when grown indoors.
Planting Group 5

Viburnum burkwoodii   Zone 5

360   Large, dark green leaves on this hardy shrub to eight feet. Large, waxy pinkish-white blooms with a delightful gardenia fragrance. Evergreen in much of California, but deciduous in colder areas.
Planting Group 1

Viburnum japonicum   Zone 8

361   A vigorous, evergreen shrub to eight or nine feet with large light green foliage. Fragrant white flowers.   Planting Group 1

Viburnum macrocephalum 'Sterile'   Zone 4
(Chinese Snowball)

362   Deciduous in the colder areas but nearly evergreen elsewhere. Bright, glossy green, eight-inch-long foliage, with flowers in clusters, six to eight inches across. Blooms in April.   Planting Group 1

363   *Viburnum odoratissimum*

365   *Viburnum tinus* 'Robustum'

Viburnum odoratissimum   Zone 7
(Sweet Viburnum)

363   Grows rapidly to ten or twelve feet and as wide. Handsome six-inch-long dark green leaves that have a varnished look. Some of the leaves, here and there all over the shrub, turn red in the fall. Fragrant white flowers in spring and summer. Prefers shade, but will grow in the sun on the coast.   Planting Group 1

Viburnum opulus 'Sterile'   Zone 4
(Snowball)

364   Deciduous. Well-known, very hardy shrub to ten feet, producing masses of round "snowballs" in May and June. Another of the few plants that produce good fall color in California. Sun.
                                                 Planting Group 1

Yucca aloifolia   Zone 8
(Spanish Dagger)

366   Slender, dagger-like leaves gives this plant a very picturesque effect. Grows to ten feet and has tall flower stems with showy clusters of white purple-tinged flowers in late spring and summer. Needs well-drained soil.
                                    Planting Group 3

Viburnum tinus 'Robustum'   Zone 6

365   An excellent dense-growing, tall shrub. In the winter, it is covered with clusters of pink buds which open to white flowers in late winter and early spring. It is taller growing and does not mildew like its parent, V. Tinus.   Planting Group 1

364   *Viburnum opulus* 'Sterile'

366   *Yucca aloifolia*

368   Yucca recurvifolia

367   Yucca gloriosa

Yucca gloriosa   Zone 8
(Soft Tip Yucca)

367   Bright gray-green foliage on this tropical-looking multi-stemmed
Yucca. Soft tips will not penetrate the skin. Over-watering may produce
black areas in the leaves.   Planting Group 3

Yucca recurvifolia (Y. pendula)   Zone 7

368   A beautiful bold accent plant that loves a dry location. Long
showy, blue-green, recurving leaves on this plant that branches with
age.   Planting Group 3

TEMPERATURE RATINGS

Zone 10	40° to 30°
Zone 9	30° to 20°
Zone 8	20° to 10°
Zone 7	10° to 0°
Zone 6	0° to -10°
Zone 5	-10° to -20°
Zone 4	-20° to -30°
Zone 3	-30° to -40°

Temperatures suggested in this book are approximate. The growing conditions,
for example, a warm late fall often will keep the plants from hardening off and
a sudden cold snap has been known to freeze plants 20° above the normal freezing
point.

TREES

370 *Acacia baileyana* 'Purpurea'

Acacia baileyana 'Purpurea'　　　　Zone 8
(Purple Leaf Acacia)

370 Evergreen, attractive, purple-tipped variety of the above. Same delightful yellow flowers but should be cut back regularly to keep producing the colored foliage. Excellent as a trimmed hedge.
　　　　　　　　　　　　Planting Group 1

369 *Acacia baileyana*

Acacia baileyana　　　　Zone 8
(Bailey Acacia or Fernleaf Acacia)

369 Evergreen. Small or medium size, fast growing tree with feathery, blue-green foliage. It is covered with a cloud of bright yellow, fuzzy flowers in the spring. Many asthma and hay fever sufferers are allergic to this widely planted tree. Grows anywhere.　　Planting Group 1

371 *Acacia longifolia*

Acacia longifolia (A. latifolia)　　　　Zone 8
(Golden Wattle)

371 Evergreen. A large bush or small tree much used as a background shrub or windbreak. Bright yellow flowers in the spring. Good at the seashore.　　　　　　　　Planting Group 1

372   *Acacia melanoxylon*

373   *Acacia verticillata*

Acacia verticillata   Zone 9
(Star Acacia)

373   Evergreen. Used mainly as a low hedge or tall bank cover to prevent trespassing. Needle-like dark green foliage that looks 'Piney' covering thorns and soft yellow flowers. Can be held at four feet as a bush but will grow to twelve feet if allowed. Withstands drought and wind.   Planting Group 1

Acacia melanoxylon   Zone 9
(Blackwood Acacia)

372   Probably the fastest growing evergreen tree in California. It reseeds itself and grows to forty feet or more. A good looking tree and were it not for this bad habit of self seeding, it would be more useful. As with the rest of the acacias, weeds (or anything else) seldom grow under it.   Planting Group 1

Acer circinatum   Zone 5
(Vine Maple)

374   Deciduous. A slender but often robust vine-like shrub or small tree to twenty feet. New foliage with reddish tints; leaves light green all summer, turning orange-scarlet or yellow in the fall. Likes a rich, moist soil. Native to Northern California and Oregon.
                                                 Planting Group 5

Acer japonicum 'Aconitifolium'   Zone 5
(Fernleaf Full Moon Maple)

375   Deciduous. A small deciduous tree, almost shrub-like, seldom more than eight feet. The leaves are deeply cut with each lobe serrated. Excellent fall coloring. Should be planted where it gets some sun, even full sun but with the roots shaded.   Planting Group 1

374   *Acer circinatum*

375   *Acer japonicum* 'Aconitifolium'

376 Acer palmatum

Acer palmatum   Zone 5

(Japanese Maple)

376 Deciduous. Small bushy tree that grows rather slowly and gracefully. Leaves are small, two inches, glistening green in summer, and rich shades of red or gold in fall. Ideal small garden tree, but cannot stand wind. Can be pruned and thinned to give special effects. Resistant to oak root fungus, therefore good as understory tree for oaks.   Planting Group 4

Acer palmatum 'Atropurpureum'   Zone 5

(Red Japanese Maple)

377 Deciduous. A small gracefully branched tree or tall shrub. New foliage is brilliant red that deepens to dark red. Prefers shaded roots in hot and dry locations. Best in Northern California areas or farther north in Oregon and Washington. Of the selected varieties, Oshio Beni or Burgundy Lace are two of the choicest.   Planting Group 5

Acer palmatum 'Sangokaku'   Zone 5

(Coral Bark Maple)

378 Deciduous. More tree-like than most varieties and in many ways very similar to A. Palmatum, but smaller. The fall foliage is yellow with a tint of rose. The new growth and the bark are a striking coral red.   Planting Group 5

378 Acer palmatum 'Sangokaku'

Acer platanoides   Zone 3

(Norway Maple)

379 Deciduous. Grows rapidly to thirty or forty feet, eventually to fifty feet making a handsome ornamental tree where there is plenty of space. It is a dense tree giving deep shade. New leaves in the spring are red; green all summer; then turns gold in the autumn.
Planting Group 1

377 Acer palmatum 'Atropurpureum'

379 Acer platanoides

380   Acer platanoides 'Schwedleri'

382   Acer saccharinum

Acer platanoides 'Crimson King'   Zone 3
(Crimson King Maple)

381   Deciduous. A patented variety of A. Schwedleri that holds its deep red purple color until fall. An excellent tree where deep red color will accent the landscape.   Planting Group 1

Acer platanoides 'Schwedleri'   Zone 3
(Schwedleri Purple Leaf Maple)

380   Deciduous. Red leaf variety of Norway Maple. Leaves stay red for a longer period than the regular Norway Maple, but turn rusty green by mid-summer.   Planting Group 2

Acer saccharinum (A. dasycarpum)   Zone 3
(Silver Maple)

382   Deciduous. The common name comes from the underside of the leaf which is silver-white, while the upper side is light green. Fast growing, to fifty feet, usually too large for a small garden. Tolerates, but is not too happy with wet soil. Beautiful for a large shade tree.   Planting Group 1

Aesculus carnea 'Briotii'   Zone 3
(Red Horsechestnut)

383   Deciduous. Rather slow growth to twenty feet; about as wide as tall. Large, divided fan-shaped leaflets making a dense shade. Flowers are bright red plumes which stand upright to about eight inches long above the foliage layer. Exceptional when in bloom.   Planting Group 1

381   Acer platanoides 'Crimson King'

383   Aesculus carnea 'Briotii'

385   *Albizia julibrissin*

384   *Aesculus hippocastanum*

Aesculus hippocastanum   Zone 3

(White Horsechestnut)

384   Deciduous. Moderate growth to fifty feet with a forty foot spread. Large deep green foliage making a dense, round-headed tree. Hundreds of upright white plumes held above the foliage in April or May.   Planting Group 1

Albizia julibrissin   Zone 7

(Silktree, Pink Acacia, Mimosa)

Alnus rhombifolia   Zone 8

(White Alder)

385   Deciduous. Grows rapidly sidewards to about twelve, then eventually to thirty feet and spreads as widely into the shape of an umbrella. Does best where it has hot summers, not too good near the coast. Not a good patio tree because of the messy flower droppings.   Planting Group 1

387   Deciduous. Tall, extremely fast growing California native tree. Dense green foliage and gray trunk. Native habitat is next to a stream, so plant this where it gets a lot of water.
                          Planting Group 2

Alnus cordata   Zone 5

(Italian Alder)

386   A strong, fast growing, deciduous thirty foot tree with a pyramidal habit of growth. Handsome glossy foliage. Can be recognized by the catkins which hang on the tree.   Planting Group 4

386   *Alnus cordata*

387   *Alnus rhombifolia*

388   *Arbutus menziesii*

Arbutus menziesii   Zone 8
(Madrone)

388   Forms a broad, round-headed evergreen tree to one hundred
feet. Bark very outstanding; a pale green changing to red. Flowers
white followed by red berries. A wonderful tree for a wild native
planting, but not too well adapted to general garden conditions.
                                              Planting Group 1

Bauhinia purpurea (B. variegata)   Zone 9
(Orchid Tree)

389   Partially to wholly deciduous. A very showy twenty foot tree
with umbrella-like crown. Slow growing, with large two to three inch
reddish-purple, fragrant flowers during winter and spring. Needs
well-drained soil. Variety B. Candida is white.   Planting Group 2

Betula alba (B. verrucosa)   Zone 2
(European White Birch)

390   Deciduous. A popular, fast growing pyramidal tree to thirty five
feet. Usually grown in groups of three or more. Lacy, light-green
foliage and beautiful white bark marked with black lines.
                                              Planting Group 1

390   *Betula alba*

Betula alba 'Laciniata'   Zone 2
(Cutleaf White Birch)

391   Deciduous. Similar to the European
White Birch, except that the main trunk is
straighter, the branches are more weeping and
the leaves deeply cut. Usually planted in groups
in lawn areas.   Planting Group 1

389   *Bauhinia purpurea*

391   *Betula alba* 'Laciniata'

393   Betula alba 'Youngii'

Betula alba 'Papyrifera'   Zone 2
(Canoe Birch, Paper Birch)

392   Deciduous. Similar to the European white birch but more open in growth, not so weeping. The bark peels off in layers. Leaves about four inches long. Like the rest of the birches, needs ample water during the summer and is susceptible to aphids so should be sprayed regularly.   Planting Group 1

392   Betula alba 'Papyrifera'

Betula alba 'Youngii' *(B. verrucosa)*   Zone 3
(Young's Weeping Birch)

393   A very decorative garden specimen that must be staked to the desired height as the branches hang straight down.
                                      Planting Group 1

Callistemon viminalis   Zone 8
(Weeping Bottlebrush)

395   Evergreen. A fast growing tree to fifteen or twenty feet with pendulous branches and bright red flowers. Must be staked when young and is not for a windy area. Planting Group 1

Callistemon lanceolatus (C. citrinus)   Zone 8
(Red Bottle Brush)

394   Evergreen tree to fifteen feet that will take a dry condition and still produce brilliant red blooms.   Planting Group 1

394   Callistemon lanceolatus

395   Callistemon viminalis

397 *Carpinus betulus* 'Columnaris'

Carpinus betulus 'Columnaris'   Zone 5
(European Hornbean)

397 Deciduous. Grows thirty to forty feet in
a dense pyramidal form. Dark green foliage,
three to four inches long, that turns yellow in
the fall.   Planting Group 1

398 *Catalpa speciosa*

396 *Camphora officinarum*

Camphora officinarum (Cinnamomum camphora)   Zone 8
(Camphor Tree)

396 Evergreen. Makes a round-headed tree not too large for a small
garden, usually about fifteen feet tall and as wide in fifteen years.
Eventually to fifty feet wide and as tall. Foliage light yellow green
with very attractive bronzy juvenile foliage. Likes a dry location.
                     Planting Group 2

Catalpa speciosa   Zone 4
(Western catalpa)

398 Deciduous. A round-headed fifty to seventy foot sub-tropical
looking tree. Extra large leaves and large clusters of two inch wide
white flowers are marked with yellow and soft green. Well adapted
to extremes of heat or cold.   Planting Group 1

Ceratonia siliqua   Zone 9
(Carob Tree or St. John's Bread)

399 Evergreen. The "breadfruit" tree of the Bible. Rounded tree
with dark green foliage to twenty feet and as wide. Ideal for street
trees in drought areas. Must be in a dry location. With garden water
the roots become shallow so it often falls over.   Planting Group 2

399 *Ceratonia siliqua*

402 *Cornus florida* 'Rubra'

400 *Chorisia speciosa*

Cornus florida 'Rubra'   Zone 4
(Pink Flowering Dogwood)

402 Deciduous. Grown for its spectacular autumn color as well as for the lovely pink "flowers" in spring. Use plenty of peat moss and leaf mold to insure an acid soil-condition. The roots should be shaded.   Planting Group 4

Cornus florida 'Welchii'   Zone 4
(Tricolor Dogwood)

403 Deciduous. Flowers on this variety are a rather inconspicuous pinkish to white so is grown for its unusual variegated foliage. The leaves, about four inches long with creamy white and pink variegation turn to deep rose, almost red, in the fall.   Planting Group 4

Chorisia speciosa   Zone 10
(Floss Silk Tree)

400 Evergreen to briefly deciduous. A spectacular tree in October, November and December when it produces masses of pink blooms. When young, a fast grower, three to five feet a year, then slowly to forty feet. The trunk, usually grass green, turns gray with age and studded with spines. Fast drainage is the key to making this one grow.   Planting Group 3

Cornus florida   Zone 4
(White Flowering Dogwood)

401 Deciduous. Small tree or large shrub for a shaded location. Likes a woodsy soil that is well-drained and has plenty of water. White "flowers" in early spring. Grown as much for the brilliant fall coloring as for the flower.   Planting Group 4

401 *Cornus florida*

403 *Cornus florida* 'Welchii'

404   *Cornus nuttallii*

406   *Crataegus cordata*

Cornus nuttallii   Zone 7
(Pacific or Western Dogwood)

404   Deciduous. One of our most spectacular
Western natives but not nearly as easy to grow
as the Eastern dogwood (C. Florida). If you
have an area where there is exceptionally good
drainage, very little summer water and shade
so the bark will not burn, it is well worth while.
Will grow to thirty feet or more.
                                    Planting Group 3

Cornus nuttallii 'Goldspot'   Zone 7
(Goldspot Dogwood)

405   Deciduous. Leaves are splashed with bright golden spots. A long
two month flowering season and often another one in the fall. This
variety blooms even as a two foot plant.   Planting Group 3

Crataegus cordata   Zone 4
(Washington Thorn)

406   Deciduous. White flowers in spring followed with clusters of
small red berries similar to Pyracantha "berries" in the fall. Grows
to twenty feet.   Planting Group 1

Crataegus lavallei (C. carrierei)   Zone 4
(Carrierei Hawthorn)

407   Deciduous. This variety grows erect to twenty-five feet and does
not spread widely. Large dark green leaves three to four inches long
and one inch wide. It is noted for its clusters of orange-red, cherry
size berries that hang on all winter.   Planting Group 1

405   *Cornus nuttallii* 'Goldspot'

407   *Crataegus lavallei*

409   *Cupaniopsis anacardioides*

Crataegus oxyacantha 'Paulii'   Zone 4
(Paul's Double Scarlet Hawthorn)

408   Deciduous. The most popular of the flowering Hawthorn family. Long sprays of double red flowers in April. Some red berries in the fall. Grows to about twenty five feet.   Planting Group 1

Cupaniopsis anacardioides   Zone 9
(Carrotwood)

409   Evergreen. An ideal tree for sub-tropical gardens. It is a clean tree, handsome in a patio, lawn or as a street tree. The compound leaves are made up of six to ten four-inch leaflets. Fragrant, greenish white flowers that turn to reddish seed pods. Stands salt wind on the coast or hot dry winds inland and grows to about forty feet.
          Planting Group 1

Diospyros kaki   Zone 8
(Persimmon)

410   Deciduous. Varieties: Hachiya, Fuyu and others. Fruit trees have been excluded from this list, but as it is one of my favorite ornamental garden trees, I have given it a place. A round-headed tree to fifteen feet with a twenty foot spread. Immense leaves to four inches wide and ten inches long that first hide the fruit, then turn into bright orange and red autumn shades. They fall exposing the beautiful salmon-orange fruit that stays on the tree until late November, when it is picked and allowed to ripen.   Planting Group 1

408   *Crataegus oxyacantha* 'Paulii'

Dodonaea viscosa 'Purpurea'   Zone 8
(Purple Leafed Hopseed Bush)

411   Evergreen shrub or tree. Attractive, fast growing small tree (or shrub) to fifteen feet, having rusty green foliage that turns to brilliant purple as soon as the cold weather arrives.
          Planting Group 1

410   *Diospyros kaki*

411   *Dodonaea viscosa* 'Purpurea'

412   Eriobotrya deflexa

418   Eucalyptus globulus 'Compacta'

413   Eriobotrya japonica

Eriobotrya deflexa (Photinia deflexa)   Zone 9
(Bronze Loquat)

412   An outstanding evergreen tree to fifteen feet. The new foliage
is a bright bronze color while mature leaves are dark green.
                                                        Planting Group 1

Eriobotrya japonica   Zone 8
(Loquat)

413   Evergreen. Tropical fruit tree. Leathery leaves to twelve inches
long and four inches wide. A tree to fifteen feet high with equal spread.
Edible yellow-orange fruit in the spring. Unfortunately, almost all
plants in the trade today are seedlings, and the quality of fruit from
one plant to the next is uncertain. It is very worth while as an
ornamental tree and is pest free.   Planting Group 1

414   Eucalpytus citriodora

Eucalpytus citriodora   Zone 9
(Lemon Scented Gum)

414   Evergreen. Moderate growth to fifty or sixty feet. A very slender
and graceful tree with a beautiful pinkish gray trunk. Often used in
groups of three, as with birch, to get a full effect. Planting Group 1

416   *Eucalyptus ficifolia*

415   *Eucalyptus ficifolia*

Eucalyptus ficifolia   Zone 9
(Red Flowering Eucalyptus)

415-416   Evergreen. A wonderful, small Eucalyptus to twenty-five feet. Great clusters of feathery scarlet flowers. All are seedling grown, and even from selected seed a small percentage will bloom pink, white, or even orange. They do not usually bloom in containers, and because of this, nurserymen cannot guarantee the color. Be careful in transplanting, as this tree resents being disturbed and readily dies if the ball is broken.   Planting Group 2

Eucalyptus globulus 'Compacta'   Zone 9
(Dwarf Blue Gum)

418   Evergreen. A dwarf, compact form of the big variety so widely planted in California. This one is used extensively for a tall hedge or wind screen spaced four to eight feet apart. Grows to twenty or thirty feet. It is bushy, has blue-gray foliage, and makes a fast screen.   Planting Group 2

Eucalyptus globulus   Zone 9
(Blue Gum)

417   Evergreen. A big robust tree widely planted on Northern California hillsides in the early 1900's. Grows to one hundred-fifty feet or more and as cities stretch out into the hill areas, more and more are found around new homes where it is almost impossible to grow an ordinary garden because of the roots.   Planting Group 1

Eucalyptus lehmannii   Zone 9
(Bushy Yate)

419   Evergreen. Winter flowering, multistem with attractive gray-green foliage and smooth white bark. Excellent low screen tree that can be kept under ten feet.   Planting Group 1

417   *Eucalyptus globulus*

419   *Eucalyptus lehmannii*

420   *Eucalyptus polyanthemos*

423   *Eucalyptus viminalis*

Eucalyptus pulverulenta   Zone 9
(Dollar Leaf Gum)

421   Evergreen. Moderate growth to twenty-five feet. Round silver-gray leaves. Best when cut back for new growth. Extensively grown for the florist trade as it is very popular for use in arrangements.
Planting Group 2

Eucalyptus polyanthemos   Zone 9
(Red Box Gum)

420   Evergreen. Small, graceful, slender tree with dollar size, round, silver-gray foliage. All the foliage is widely used for indoor decoration. Should be heavily pruned and kept below ten feet.   Planting Group 2

Eucalyptus sideroxylon 'Rosea'   Zone 9
(Red Iron Bark)

422   Evergreen. Slow moderate growth to forty feet. The tree is slim and airy in appearance with bluish-green foliage turning bronze in the winter. Masses of pink blossoms in spring and summer.
Planting Group 2

421   *Eucalyptus pulverulenta*

422   *Eucalyptus sideroxylon* 'Rosea'

426   *Fagus sylvatica* 'Tricolor'

424   *Fagus sylvatica*

Eucalyptus viminalis   Zone 8
(Ribbon Gum)

423   Evergreen. A fast growing graceful tree with pendulous white
flowers and very attractive smooth white bark.   Planting Group 1

Flowering Crabapple   See Malus
Flowering Cherry   See Prunus
Flowering Peach   See Prunus

Fagus sylvatica 'Tricolor'   Zone 4
(Tricolor Beech)

426   Deciduous. Glossy green leaves marked
with white and edged pink. Slow to about
twenty five feet. The trunk burns in very hot
sun or warm dry winds. Do not allow it to
completely dry out.   Planting Group 1

Fagus sylvatica   Zone 4
(European Beech)

424   Deciduous tree to seventy feet with a broad cone on top while
the lower branches reach to the ground. The foliage is dark glossy
green. A good lawn tree, but needs space to look its best.
                                        Planting Group 1

Fagus sylvatica 'Atropunicea'   Zone 4
(Copper Beech)

425   Deciduous. Good in all except the hot interior where the trunk
is subject to sun burn. Valuable because of its purple foliage. All
plants in the trade are grafted and a mature tree may reach fifty
feet.   Planting Group 1

425   *Fagus sylvatica* 'Atropunicea'

428   Ficus elastica 'Decora'

Fiscus elastica 'Decora'   Zone 9
(Rubber Tree)

428   Evergreen. Usually grown indoors except
in Southern California and known as the Rubber Tree. Large, bold, glossy dark green leaves.
Excellent when planted in protected areas or
as a tubbed plant.   Planting Group 2

427   Ficus benjamina

Ficus benjamina   Zone 10
(Weeping Fig)

427   Evergreen. An outstanding "Ficus" that can grow outdoors in
full sun in parts of California or can be grown indoors and will stand
pruning. It has rich green foliage and pleasing weeping appearance.
Excellent container plant.   Planting Group 1

Ficus retusa nitida   Zone 9
(Indian Laurel)

429   Evergreen. Excellent small tree for street use or as a tubbed
specimen. Often grown as a pyramid or a patio tree (Globe). Handsome, thick rubbery green foliage and the plant stands pruning. In
Southern California many trees will reach thirty feet.

Planting Group 2

Fraxinus uhdei   Zone 9
(Shamel Ash)

430   Evergreen. Excellent fast growing round
headed shade tree to forty feet. Has dark glossy
green leaves. Do not plant near a sidewalk as
this plant is shallow rooted. Planting Group 2

429   Ficus retusa nitida

430   Fraxinus uhdei

431 *Fraxinus velutina* 'Glabra'

Fraxinus velutina 'Glabra'   Zone 6
(Modesto Ash)

431 Medium size deciduous tree to fifty feet. A sturdy, fast growing, round headed tree especially suited for warmer areas as a shade tree. Fall bonus with this tree as leaves turn to golden yellow before dropping.   Planting Group 1

Gleditsia triacanthos inermis   Zone 4
(Honey Locust)

433 Deciduous. A thornless, fast growing slender tree to seventy feet. Excellent for the desert or any harsh growing location where it is hot.   Planting Group 1

Gleditsia triacanthos 'Moraine'   Zone 4
(Moraine Locust)

434 Deciduous. One of the fastest growing shade trees (to fifty feet) in the trade today. Ideal hot country shade tree, some flowers, clean habits and good form.   Planting Group 1

432 *Ginkgo biloba*

Ginkgo biloba   Zone 4
(Maidenhair Tree)

432 Deciduous. Large tree with spreading open habit to seventy feet but usually only about forty feet. Leaves are flat and fan shaped, soft clear green in color, turning to soft yellow in the fall. Many trees sold in nurseries are seedlings. The females develop fruit in sufficient quantities to cover the ground. The fruit has a very disagreeable odor and is very messy. One should buy a named variety such as "Autumn Gold" or "Palo Alto" which are grafted and are male plants with excellent color in the fall, but without messy fruit drop.
                          Planting Group 1

433 *Gleditsia triacanthos inermis*

434 *Gleditsia triacanthos* 'Moraine'

435   *Gleditsia triacanthos* 'Shademaster'

436   *Gleditsia triacanthos* 'Sunburst'

Gleditsia triacanthos 'Shademaster'   Zone 4
(Shademaster Locust)

435   Deciduous. This large shade tree needs plenty of room. It is
as hardy and as tolerant as the other Honey Locust but grows faster,
wider and has larger leaves. Grows to fifty feet or more.
                                                        Planting Group 1

Gleditsia triacanthos 'Sunburst'   Zone 4
(Sunburst Locust)

436   A deciduous tree to forty feet. This one needs full sun to be
at its best and show its golden yellow crown of graceful delicate foliage.   Planting Group 1

Grevillea robusta   Zone 9
(Silk Oak)

437   Evergreen. Tall, narrow tree to sixty feet with finely divided
fern-like deep green foliage. Four inch golden yellow flower trusses
are borne in profusion in the spring. Unfortunately, the tree drops
leaves the year around so is somewat messy.   Planting Group 1

Harpephyllum caffrum   Zone 10
(Kafir Plum)

438   Attractive, fast growing, evergreen shade tree to thirty feet with
luxuriant dark green foliage. The new growth is tinted with red.
Produces a small dark red edible fruit. Does best in warmer coastal
areas and prefers light, moist, well drained soil.   Planting Group 1

437   *Grevillea robusta*

438   *Harpephyllum caffrum*

441 *Jacaranda mimosaefolia*

Hymenosporum flavum   Zone 9
(Sweetshade)

439 Evergreen. Small tree to twenty feet or large shrub with a slender, upright habit of growth. Shiny, dark green foliage and clusters of very fragrant light orange flowers in the early summer. Somewhat tender.   Planting Group 3

Ilex altaclarensis 'Wilsonii'   Zone 6

440 One of the finest large evergreen hollies. Large dark green foliage, spiny thick leaves and large bright red berries. Ideal as a large shrub or small tree.   Planting Group 1

Jacaranda mimosaefolia (J. acutifolia)   Zone 9
(Jacaranda)

441 Semi deciduous. Somewhat tender, medium-sized tree with a fern-like foliage and clusters of lavender-blue flowers. Likes a very dry location and sandy soil. Does not like wind. If you have the right location, this tree is spectacular.   Planting Group 2

439 *Hymenosporum flavum*

Koelreuteria bipinnata   Zone 8
(Chinese Flame Tree)

443 Slow to moderate growth to thirty feet and spreading. Leaves two feet long divided into leaflets. Flowers turn into capsules about two inches long and hang in large clusters about a foot in diameter and two feet long. Very showy in late summer and fall. Deep rooted and a good tree to plant under.   Planting Group 1

443 *Koelreuteria bipinnata*

440 *Ilex altaclarensis* 'Wilsonii'

445   Laburnum watereri vossii

444   Koelreuteria paniculata

Laburnum watereri 'Vossii'   Zone 5
(Golden Chain Tree)

445   Deciduous. It is best where it experiences a cold winter. Small, narrow tree to fifteen feet with bright green, compound (clover-like) foliage, and long (ten to twenty inch) clusters of bright yellow flowers that remind one of Wisteria.   Planting Group 2

Koelreuteria paniculata   Zone 6
(Golden Rain Tree)

444   An open growing deciduous tree to thirty feet that turns a beautiful yellow in the autumn. In July and August, long twelve inch pannicles of yellow flowers make this a most interesting tree. Takes heat, cold, drought, wind or alkaline soil.   Planting Group 1

Ligustrum japonicum   Zone 7
(Japanese Privet)

446   Another fast growing, evergreen plant grown both as a shrub or tree, seldom more than twenty feet. Attractive deep green foliage and fragrant white flowers in the spring. (Causes hay-fever for many). Stands heavy pruning.   Planting Group 1

Liquidambar styraciflua   Zone 5
(Sweetgum)

447   Deciduous. What Easterners miss most in California (and the natives do not blame them) is the fall coloring. The Liquidambar is one of the few trees that we can depend on to give the beautiful fall colors in red and yellow. Grows as a narrow, pyramid with branches beautifully spread to seventy feet. Leaves maple shaped. Excellent for a lawn specimen. Stands seashore.   Planting Group 1

447   Liquidambar styraciflua

446   Liqustrum japonicum

448   Liquidambar styraciflua 'Burgundy'

449   Liquidambar styraciflua 'Palo Alto'

Liquidambar styraciflua 'Burgundy'   Zone 5
448   This grafted variety has been selected and named because of
its rich burgundy red color in the autumn.   Planting Group 1

Liquidambar styraciflua 'Palo Alto'   Zone 5
449   A strain selected for its bright red leaves. All plants are grafted,
so slightly higher in price than the seedling-grown Liquidambar Styraciflua.   Planting Group 1

Liriodendron tulipifera   Zone 4
(Tulip Tree)

450   Deciduous. Fairly fast to fifty or sixty feet, symmetrical with
a straight trunk, and dark green leaves. Flowers are greenish white,
and cup-shaped. A very desirable shade tree but needs water in summer. Will not stand alkali or summer drought. Another tree with yellow or yellow brown fall color in the Southern latitudes.
                                                     Planting Group 1

Lyonothamnus floribundus   Zone 9
(Catalina Ironwood)

451   A wonderful fast growing California native evergreen tree to
thirty feet, adaptable to coastal conditions only. Attractive dark-green
fern-like foliage. The reddish-brown bark peels off in long ribbons.
The leaves keep when cut and are used in floral arrangements. The
spent flowers hang on for a long time. It is wind resistant, but should
be planted in a dry, well drained location.   Planting Group 3

450   Liriodendron tulipifera

451   Lyonothamnus floribundus

454   *Magnolia grandiflora* 'Samuel Sommer'

Magnolia grandiflora 'Samuel Sommer'
Zone 7

454   Evergreen to fifty feet. Considered by many to be the finest evergreen magnolia. The large white flowers, up to fourteen inches across, are extremely fragrant.
Planting Group 1

452   *Magnolia grandiflora*

Magnolia grandiflora
(Southern Magnolia)
Zone 7

452   Evergreen. Moderately fast growing tree with very large, dark green, shiny leaves. Flowers are white, large, and waxy. One of the most magnificent trees in the trade today. Eventually a large tree with a fifty foot spread, but it takes about fifteen to twenty-five years before it becomes too large for a city garden. Grows faster with lots of water if well drained.
Planting Group 1

Magnolia grandiflora 'St. Marys'
Zone 7

453   Evergreen. A small, especially desirable tree that looks like M. Grandiflora, but dwarf to eighteen or twenty feet. Leaves glossy deep green above and brownish underneath, flowers up to twelve inches, flowering even when young. Likes summer water.   Planting Group 1

Magnolia grandiflora 'Russet'
Zone 7

452-A   Evergreen to fifty feet. Another outstanding variety with somewhat smaller leaves and rapid pyramidal growth. The branches are more compact and the leaves are dense. The reverse side of the leaves are russet brown.
Planting Group 1

453   *Magnolia grandiflora* 'St. Marys'

452-A   *Magnolia grandiflora* 'Russet'

MALUS

(Flowering Crabapple Trees)

All are deciduous and seldom more than twenty feet tall. These are some of the most spectacular flowering trees in the trade.

455	Malus 'Almey'	Single red flowers, scarlet fruit.
456	Malus 'Arnoldiana'	A broad spreading growth with arching branches. Flowers are single pink fading to white.
457	Malus 'Bechtel'	Soft green foliage; large, double pink blooms. Last to bloom.
458	Malus 'Dorothea'	Semi-double pink flowers with yellow fruit. Not shown.
459	Malus 'Eleyi'	Purple red blooms. Red leaves.
460	Malus floribunda	Flowers fairly large, apple-blossom.
461	Malus 'Hopa'	Fast growing, upright; leaves dark green with a brownish cast. Flowers rose red.
462	Malus 'Katherine'	Large, two inch double, bluish pink flowers.
463	Malus kaido (Parkmani)	Early, showy pink flowers and small red fruit. Not shown.
464	Malus 'Scheideckeri'	Semi-double, rose pink and small yellow fruit.
465	Malus 'Snowdrift'	Pink bud and large single white flowers.

Zone 4

455   Malus 'Almey'

456   Malus 'Arnoldiana'

457   Malus 'Bechtel'

459   Malus 'Eleyi'

460   *Malus floribunda*

462   *Malus* 'Katherine'

461   *Malus* 'Hopa'

464   *Malus* 'Scheideckeri'

465   *Malus* 'Snowdrift'

466   *Maytenus boaria*

Maytenus boaria   Zone 8
(Mayten Tree)

466   Evergreen. Moderate growth to fifteen feet, then slow to twenty
or twenty-five feet. Long pendulous branches remind one of a small
weeping willow. Excellent small garden tree.   Planting Group 2

467   *Melaleuca linariifolia*

Melaleuca linariifolia   Zone 9
(Flaxleaf Paperbark)

467   A small evergreen tree to thirty feet with
bright green needle-like foliage and fluffy spikes
of small white flowers.   Planting Group 1

Melaleuca leucadendra   Zone 9
(Cajeput Tree, Swamp Tea Tree)

468   Excellent evergreen tree to twenty feet or large shrub with a
distinctive spongy light colored bark. Rich green foliage and slender
spikes of white, yellow, pink or purple flowers.   Planting Group 1

Melia azedarach 'Umbraculiformis'   Zone 8
(Texas Umbrella Tree)

469   Excellent deciduous shade tree to forty feet in hot climates. Will
grow almost anywhere, growing rapidly in average soils. Nice clusters
of lavender flowers in the spring followed by green berries.
                                            Planting Group 1

469   *Melia azedarach* 'Umbraculiformis'

468   *Melaleuca leucadendra*

471   Morus alba 'Fruitless'

470   Metrosideros tomentosa

Morus alba 'Fruitless'   Zone 5
(Fruitless Mulberry)

471   Deciduous. A very fast growing tree to thirty or forty feet with
as wide a spread. Large, shiny, dark green leaves and no fruit. Stands
heat, drought, alkali soil, and neglect. Prune carefully when young
as rapid, spindly growth can lead to frequent breaking of brittle
wood.   Planting Group 1

Metrosideros tomentosa (M. excelsas)   Zone 9
(New Zealand Christmas Tree)

470   Evergreen. Excellent tree for coastal planting to about thirty feet.
Will stand the wind as well as salt spray and ocean salt water at
the roots. Thick glossy oblong attractive leaves, dark gray on top,
gray underneath. Large dark crimson flowers in clusters in June and
July.   Planting Group 1

472   Myoporum laetum

Myoporum laetum   Zone 9

472   Evergreen. A fast growing large shrub often grown in tree form
to twenty feet. Well adapted to wind swept coastal areas and drought
conditions. Has thick, leathery (almost succulent-like) deep green foliage.   Planting Group 1

473   Olea europaea

Olea europaea 'Mission'   Zone 8
(Mission Olive)

473   Evergreen. Extremely drought resistant once established. Gray-
green foliage and picturesque gnarled trunks on older specimens that
reach a height of twenty feet.   Planting Group 1

Oxydendrum arboreum   Zone 5
(Sourwood Tree or Sorreltree)

474   Deciduous. The five to eight inch leaves turn a brilliant scarlet
in the fall. In the summer it has clusters of Andromeda-like, creamy
white flowers. Usually found in the Northwest. Grows to fifty feet,
needs acid soil.   Planting Group 1

474   *Oxydendrum arboreum*

475   *Photinia* 'Fraseri'

Photinia 'Fraseri'   Zone 7

475   Evergreen. Grown both as a large shrub or small tree to twenty feet. The new foliage has brilliant red leaves as well as red stems. In the spring, showy clusters of white flowers. This variety is more mildew resistant than most Photinias.   Planting Group 1

Pistacia chinensis   Zone 7

(Pistachio)

476   Deciduous. A beautiful shade tree growing to fifty or sixty feet. Leaves, similar to our native Black Walnut, turn a vivid red-yellow and orange in the fall. It is best where it is hot and well watered in the summer.   Planting Group 1

Pittosporum undulatum   Zone 9

(Victoria Box)

477   Evergreen. Small, round-headed tree or shrub to twenty feet or more. Dark green, glossy six-inch leaves, fragrant, creamy-white flowers followed by orange berries. Fast growing. Stands considerable drought. Must be trained to tree form when young.
          Planting Group 1

476   *Pistacia chinensis*

477   *Pittosporum undulatum*

478   Platanus acerifolia

Platanus acerifolia   Zone 7
(European Sycamore or London Plane)

478   Deciduous. Large handsome street or
shade tree to seventy feet. Leaves are large,
dense and bright green. It is tough and rugged,
and tolerant of almost any soil condition.
                                    Planting Group 1

479   Platanus occidentalis

Platanus occidentalis   Zone 6
(American Sycamore)

479   A very rapid growing deciduous Sycamore with an unusually
large trunk. This one is for the "country" only, as it does not like
the city air; otherwise almost the same as the "London Plane". Grows
to fifty feet.   Planting Group 1

Platanus racemosa   Zone 7
(California Sycamore)

480   Deciduous. This California native, often up to one hundred feet,
has large Maple-like leaves. It is not a thick dense tree as is P. acerifolia.
The bark is grayish and mottled. Often grown in clumps at an angle.
Picturesque.   Planting Group 1

Podocarpus elongatus gracilior   Zone 9
(Fern Podocarpus)

481   Evergreen. This fern-like conifer grows to a medium sized tree
and is one of the most graceful plants we have in the trade. Can
be kept to any size desired by pruning and will grow in full shade
or full sun or indoors, but wants a well-drained location without too
much water.   Planting Group 3

480   Platanus racemosa

481   Podocarpus elongatus gracilior

Populus nigra 'Italica' Zone 4
(Lombardy Poplar)

482 Deciduous. Fast and columnar to seventy-five feet or more. Excellent windbreak for farmland, but requires too much space for a city lot. Keep away from sewers and septic tanks. Beautiful in the fall when leaves turn bright yellow before dropping.
Planting Group 1

FLOWERING PLUM

Prunus cerasifera Zone 5
Grown both for the brilliant red or purplish red foliage as well as the flowers. All deciduous.

483 *Prunus cerasifera* 'Blireiana'
Foliage reddish green. A showy double pink that flowers early. No fruit.

484 *Prunus cerasifera* 'Hollywood'
Leaves dark green above, red underneath. Flowers pink to white. Good quality fruit.

485 *Prunus cerasifera* 'Pissardii'
Purple leaf. Single delicate pink flower followed by reddish fruit. Flower of *P. Pissardii* has only a faint blush of pink in early stages then clear white as it gets fully open.

486 *Prunus cerasifera* 'Thundercloud'
Deep purple leaf, single delicate pink blooms. Some fruit.

487 *Prunus cerasifera* 'Thundercloud'
In flower. No fruit.

482 *Populus nigra* 'Italica'

485 *Prunus cerasifera* 'Pissardii'

483 *Prunus cerasifera* 'Blireiana'

486   *Prunus cerasifera* 'Thundercloud'

487   *Prunus cerasifera* 'Thundercloud'

FLOWERING PEACH

Prunus persica   Zone 5

Deciduous and seldom more than fifteen feet in height. Identical in growing and habit to fruiting peach. Heavy pruning when in flower or immediately after for a good show of flowers the following year. Many named varieties in the trade but usually found in nurseries as double Red, Pink, White or Variegated; all in early and late flowering varieties.

Planting Group 1.

488   *Prunus persica* Double white

489   *Prunus persica* Double red

490   *Prunus persica* Double pink

488   *Prunus persica* Double white

490   *Prunus persica* Double pink

489   *Prunus persica* Double red

FLOWERING CHERRY

FLOWERING CHERRY   Zone 5

491   *Prunus serrulata* 'Akebono' *(Daybreak)*
      Single, pale pink flower and spreading form. (Often called
      the most beautiful flowering tree in the world).

492   *Prunus serrulata* 'Amanogawa'
      Columnar. Semi-double, soft pink flowers.

492 A   *Prunus serrulata* 'Beni Hoshi'
      Arching growth; vivid, single pink flowers.

493   *Prunus serrulata* 'Kwanzan'
      Upright growth; large, double, deep pink.

494   *Prunus serrulata* 'Naden'
      Upright growth; semi-double, soft pink.

495   *Prunus serrulata* 'Shirotae' *(Mt. Fuji)*
      Pure double white.

496   *Prunus serrulata* 'Yoshino' *(Yedoensis)*
      Fragrant single white, early.

497   *Prunus subhirtella Weeping form* Double pink, drooping form.

498   *Prunus subhirtella Weeping form* Single pink, drooping form.

499   *Prunus subhirtella Weeping form* Double pink, arching growth.

                           Planting Group 1.

492   Prunus serrulata 'Amanogawa'

492A   Prunus serrulata 'Beni Hoshi'

491   Prunus serrulata 'Akebono' *(Daybreak)*

493   Prunus serrulata 'Kawanzan'

494   *Prunus serrulata* 'Naden'

495   *Prunus serrulata* 'Shirotae' *(Mt. Fuji)*

496   *Prunus serrulata* 'Yoshino' *(Yedoensis)*

497   *Prunus subhirtella Weeping, Double pink, drooping form.*

498   *Prunus subhirtella Weeping Single pink, drooping form.*

499   *Prunus subhirtella Weeping Double pink, arching growth.*

501   Pyrus kawakamii

500   Pyrus calleryana 'Bradfordi'

Pyrus calleryana 'Bradfordi'   Zone 5
(Bradford Pear)

500   Deciduous. A vigorous growing, dense-headed medium size shade tree with rich green wavy foliage and attractive scarlet color in the fall. Dense clusters of white flowers in early spring. No fruit.
                                                    Planting Group 1

Quercus coccinea   Zone 7
(Scarlet Oak)

503   Deciduous. Grows to sixty feet or more with a wide spread and a light open pattern of branches. Bright green, six-inch deeply lobed leaves that turn brilliant scarlet in the fall. Likes deep rich soil. Cut branches are sold by florists. A must if you want fall coloring and have the space.   Planting Group 1

Pyrus kawakamii   Zone 8
(Evergreen Pear)

501   Evergreen. Grows fast to thirty feet and requires constant pruning to keep it attractive as a tree. This bad habit, of course, helps when the tree is espaliered against a wall or fence. Bright, shiny foliage and fragrant white flowers. No fruit.   Planting Group 1

Quercus agrifolia   Zone 7
(Coast Live Oak)

502   Evergreen. This native California Live Oak is slow to fifty feet. Leaves small, oval and rich green. Requires a well-drained location and should not have much, if any summer water. Around new homes one must be careful not to change the soil level, and must be careful not to dam up a planting area with a driveway that does not provide rapid drainage.   Planting Group 1

502   Quercus agrifolia

503   Quercus coccinea

504   *Quercus ilex*

506   *Quercus suber*

Quercus ilex   Zone 8
(Holly Oak)

504   Evergreen. Moderately fast growth to
forty feet with round-spreading head. Clean,
dark green, glossy foliage. Faster and straighter
growing than the California Live Oak, and
rapidly replacing it in the nursery trade. Grows
very well inland as well as on the coast where
it stands salt air and wind. Almost pest free.
Excellent street tree.   Planting Group 1

Quercus palustris   Zone 4
(Pin Oak)

505   Deciduous to eighty feet. Dark green foliage turning to a showy
scarlet in the fall. Large symmetrical pyramid when young, open and
irregular when mature.   Planting Group 1

Quercus suber   Zone 9
(Cork Oak)

506   Evergreen. Native to the Mediterranean. The interesting thing
about this tree is the bark. (This is the cork of commerce). The
three-inch toothed leaves are shining dark green above and gray
beneath. Needs good drainage and can take considerable drought when
established. A good shade tree to sixty feet if in the right place.
                    Planting Group 3

Robina pseudoacacia 'Decaisneana'   Zone 1
(Pink Locust)

507   Deciduous. Tall, rapid growing to fifty feet. A variety of Black
Locust with long racemes or fragrant light pink flowers. Tolerant of
summer heat and of cold. Will stand alkaline or any other kind of
soil.   Planting Group 1

505   *Quercus palustris*

507   *Robina pseudoacacia* 'Decaisneana'

508   Salix babylonica

Salix babylonica   Zone 5
(Weeping Willow)

508   Deciduous. Fast growing, very graceful tree to thirty feet with long drooping branches. Long, narrow, bright light green leaves. Be careful where you place this one as almost nothing will grow under it, the roots take everything. It has been said this tree will dry up a swamp. Keep away from sewer lines.   Planting Group 1

509   Salix matsudana 'Tortuosa'

Salix matsudana 'Tortuosa'   Zone 3
(Corkscrew Willow)

509   Deciduous. Grows to twenty five feet or more with the branches twisted into interesting spiralling, upright patterns. Branches, both with or without leaves, are excellent for flower arrangements.
                    Planting Group 1

Schinus terebinthifolius   Zone 8
(Brazilian Pepper)

511   Evergreen. Medium sized tree to twenty feet. Leaves are larger, rounder, veined, and darker green than S. Molle, and it is a much better all around tree in the garden. Useful for shade in a small garden. Does as well on the coast as in the interior. Takes lawn water.
                    Planting Group 2

Schinus molle   Zone 8
(California Pepper Tree)

510   Evergreen. Fast growing to twenty-five feet with picturesque gnarled trunk, and long graceful weeping branches. Hardy, thrives best in poor light soil and where there is plenty of heat and little water.   Planting Group 2

510   Schinus molle

511   Schinus terebinthifolius

512   *Sorbus aucuparia*

513   *Stenocarpus sinuatus*

Sorbus aucuparia   Zone 6
(European Mountain Ash)

512   Deciduous to sixty feet. A tree best for the Northern parts where winters are colder. Broad, flat, three to five inch clusters of white flowers followed by bright orange-red one-quarter inch berries which color in midsummer and hang on until midspring unless the birds get them. Needs good drainage, should have full sun, but will take part shade.   Planting Group 3

Stenocarpus sinuatus   Zone 10
(Firewheel Tree)

513   Evergreen. Lovely tree to fifty feet that prefers an acid soil. Great masses of three to four-inch wheel-shaped, brilliant orange-red flowers in the spring. Dark green oak-like foliage. Excellent for tropical gardens in our warmer areas.   Planting Group 3

Sterculia diversifolia (Brachychiton populneum)   Zone 9
(Kurra Jong Bottle Tree)

514   Semi-evergreen tree to thirty feet with dense head and a nice compact habit. The trunk, starting at the ground is unusually thick. Yellowish flowers in summer. This one likes a hot, dry climate. Leaves always look a rich glossy green.   Planting Group 1

514   *Sterculia diversifolia*

515   *Tilia cordata*

518 *Ulmus glabra* 'Camperdownii'

Tilia cordata   Zone 3

(Little Leaf Linden)

515 Deciduous. A cold weather plant. Small leathery foliage, rapid growth in symmetrical form to forty feet. Spicy fragrant blooms.
                                    Planting Group 1

Tristania conferta   Zone 9

(Brisbane Box)

516 Evergreen. A pyramidal evergreen tree to fifty feet that likes plenty of heat and withstands drought. Looks somewhat like a Eucalyptus. Fast growing, dark green foliage, and small clusters of white flowers add to its attractiveness.   Planting Group 1

Tristania laurina   Zone 9

517 A slow growing, formal small tree or shrub to ten feet. Leaves are narrow and about four inches long making a dense, rounded crown. Flowers are clusters of yellow borne, in late spring. Evergreen.
                                    Planting Group 1

Ulmus glabra 'Camperdownii'   Zone 1

(Camperdown Weeping Elm)

518 This interesting, weeping tree will grow to about ten or twelve feet and as broad with branches that reach the ground making a tent of shade. Very scarce in the trade.   Planting Group 1

519 *Ulmus parvifolia*

516 *Tristania conferta*

Ulmus parvifolia (U. semperivirens) Zone 7

(Evergreen Elm)

519 Evergreen to about twenty-three degrees, then deciduous. A thirty foot tree with a rounded-head and graceful, arching branches. Needs pruning every winter.   Planting Group 1

517 *Tristania laurina*

520   *Ulmus parvifolia* 'Brea'

521   *Zelkova serrata*

Zelkova serrata   Zone 5
(Sawleaf Zelkova)

521   Deciduous. Fast growth to seventy-five feet. Dark green, two to five inch leaves are sharply saw-toothed and turn red in the fall. Better adapted to the hot interior than the coast. An excellent, pest-free tree where there is room.   Planting Group 1

Ulmus parvifolia 'Brea'   Zone 7
(Chinese Evergreen Elm)

520   Evergreen above thirty degrees fahrenheit then deciduous. This differs from U. Parvifolia in its growth habit, being more or less in an upright, umbrella-like form rather than drooping and much stronger growth to thirty feet.
Planting Group 1

PLANTING GUIDE

Following each description is a planting group guide. Here again, individual conditions will vary so the planting instructions are general. An attempt has been made to give you a clue to the general soil conditions needed for each plant. You should check local conditions with your nurseryman.

Group 1 means the plant will grow in the sun without special treatment, unless otherwise mentioned.

Group 2 means the plant will grow in the sun, but must have excellent drainage.

Group 3 means the plant will grow in the sun, but must have excellent drainage and only minimum amounts of water, usually gray foliage plants.

Group 4 means the plant will grow in the shade, without special treatment.

Group 5 means the plant will grow in the shade, but must have excellent drainage and special soil mixture.

VINES

All vines evergreen unless otherwise mentioned.

Ampelopsis quinquefolia (Parthenocissus quinquefolia)
Zone 4

(Virginia Creeper)

522 Deciduous. A fine, fast growing deciduous vine with large five-fingered leaves turning brilliant scarlet in the fall. It will grow on any wall.
Planting Group 1

Ampelopsis tricuspidata (Parthenocissus tricuspidata)
'Veitchii'
Zone 4

(Boston Ivy)

523 Deciduous. Close-clinging vine especially suited to cover masonry walls. Pointed leaves with delicate, light green foliage which turns brilliant red in the fall.
Planting Group 1

523   Ampelopsis tricuspidata

Beaumontia grandiflora   Zone 10
(Easter Lily Vine)

524   A beautiful vine for only the warmer parts of California. Large, dark green, six-inch leaves are smooth and shiny and furnish a tropical look. Blooms from April until September with fragrant, trumpet-like four to five inch long white flowers that look like Easter lilies. Needs deep, rich soil, ample water, and regular feeding. Planting Group 1

524   Beaumontia grandiflora

522   Ampelopsis quinquefolia

525   Bignonia cherere

Bignonia venusta (Pyrostegia venusta)   Zone 10
(Flame Vine)

526   A fast growing evergreen vine with brilliant orange trumpet shaped flowers that hang in masses during the winter months. Likes the heat of the desert.   Planting Group 1

527   Bignonia violacea

Bougainvillea 'Barbara Karst'   Zone 9
528   Evergreen. Producing more blooms than any other variety. The larger red flower bracts are produced in massive clusters continuously during warm weather. It likes rich soil but plant in full sun and keep on the dry side.   Planting Group 3

Bignonia cherere (Phaedranthus buccinatorius)   Zone 9
(Scarlet Trumpet Vine)

525   A beautiful evergreen vine that will take only a light frost. Makes a very heavy, quick cover with clusters of four-inch, bright red, tubular flowers having yellow throats. Blooms sporadically throughout the year when the weather warms. Stands heavy pruning. Feed and water regularly for best results.   Planting Group 1

526   Bignonia venusta

Bignonia violacea (Clytostoma callistegioides)   Zone 9
(Lavender Trumpet Vine)

527   Evergreen. Strong grower, either in sun or shade. Big sprays of three-inch lavender-violet trumpets on all the tip ends, literally covering the foliage from April to July. Excellent for covering fences, but needs support on a wall.   Planting Group 1

528   Bougainvillea 'Barbara Karst'

Bougainvilleas

In all, more than twenty varieties are grown in California, white, pink, red, orange and many double varieties. However only a few are found in most nurseries. Be careful when planting. Do not disturb the roots when removing the plant from the container.

532   Bougainvillea 'San Diego Red'

529   Bougainvillea 'Brasiliensis'

530   Bougainvillea 'California Gold'

531   Bougainvillea 'Orange King'

Bougainvillea 'Brasiliensis' *(B. spectabilis)*   Zone 9

529   Evergreen. An indescribable mass of color with great clusters of lavender-purple flower bracts. This tropical likes a hot wall with reflected heat. Needs support and dry feet.   Planting Group 3

Bougainvillea 'California Gold'   Zone 9

530   Vigorous evergreen vine with golden yellow "flowers" holding for many months. Do not overwater.   Planting Group 3

Bougainvillea 'Orange King'   Zone 9

531   Attractive sprays of bronzy-orange flowers produced in great abundance during the warm months along with very attractive foliage make this an outstanding plant in warm weather areas.

Planting Group 3

Bougainvillea 'San Diego Red'   Zone 9

(Scarlet O'Hara)
532   One of the most vigorous of all the Bougainvilleas. Deep crimson flowers that do not fade and are born in large clusters. One of the hardiest.   Planting Group 3

533   *Bougainvillea* 'Manila Red'

535   *Campsis tagliabuana*

Bougainvillea 'Manila Red'   Zone 10

533   One of the newer double varieties. This is one of a number of
double varieties which have been introduced but are still very scarce
in the trade.   Planting Group 3

Bougainvillea 'Temple of Fire'   Zone 9

534   A low growing, spreading bush form with exceptional fiery red
bracts.   Planting Group 3

Cissus antarctica   Zone 9
(Kangaroo Ivy)

536   An evergreen vine, fast growing and deep
green in color. Widely grown as an indoor plant
in the cooler areas and outdoors in warmer
areas.   Planting Group 1 or 4

Campsis tagliabuana   Zone 6
(Trumpet Creeper)

535   Deciduous. A vigorous climbing vine that will cling to most
surfaces and produce loose arching sprays of trumpet-shaped red
flowers. Provides excellent screen. Also grown as a shrub in clump
form.   Planting Group 1

534   *Bougainvillea* 'Temple of Fire'

536   *Cissus antarctica*

Cissus capensis (Rhoicissus capensis, Vitis capensis) Zone 10

(Evergreen Grape)

537   In the warmer areas, a fine, fast growing evergreen vine with leaves up to eight inches. Used as a ground cover or fence vine. Sun or shade.   Planting Group 1 or 4

537   Cissus capensis

Cissus rhombifolia (Vitis rhombifolia)   Zone 10

(Grape Ivy)

538   A fast growing evergreen vine with glossy foliage. Often used in a hanging basket both indoors and out.   Planting Group 4

538   Cissus rhombifolia

Clematis armandii   Zone 8

539   Evergreen. A spectacular, fast growing vine with beautiful clusters of fragrant, star-like white flowers that stand out against the dark green background of the foliage. Great on fences, a trellis or walls. Keep the roots shaded and cool.   Planting Group 4

539   Clematis armandii

Clematis

A large group of vines, mostly deciduous and all having attractive flowers. Some are most spectacular. Best in the northwest or coastal Northern California. It is one plant that should be planted deeper (two inches) than in the nursery and requires a neutral soil. It also likes a sunny location with roots in the shade.

540A   *Clematis* 'Ernest Markham'

Deciduous varieties

Clematis 'Daniel Deronda'	Large lavender pink with stripes
Clematis 'Duchess of Edinburgh'	Double white
Clematis 'Ernest Markham'	Bright cerise-red, light stamens
Clematis 'Gypsy Queen'	Deep purple
Clematis 'Henryi'	Pure white, dark stamens
Clematis 'Jackmanii'	Deep royal purple
Clematis 'Lanuginosa Candida'	Large white, light stamens
Clematis 'Mme Edward Andre'	Wine red
Clematis 'Montana Rubens'	Fragrant rose to pink
Clematis 'Mrs Cholmondeley'	Large light blue, light stamens
Clematis 'Nellie Moser'	Pink and white
Clematis 'Pink Chiffon'	Shell-pink, dark stamens
Clematis 'President'	Royal purple
Clematis 'Ramona'	Light blue

and many others.

Planting Group 1

540B   *Clematis* 'Mrs. Cholmondeley'

540C   *Clematis* 'Danial Deronda'

540D *Clematis* 'Lanuginosa Candida'

540E *Clematis* 'Henryi'

540F *Clematis* 'Nellie Mosher'

540G *Clematis* 'Ernest Markham'

540H *Clematis* 'Mrs. Cholmondeley'

540I *Clematis* 'Pink Chiffon'

540J *Clematis* 'Jackmanii'

540K *Clematis* 'Villa de Lyon'

541   Ficus repens

542   Fatshedera lizei

543   Gelsemium sempervirens

544   Hedera canariensis

Fatshedera lizei (Fatsia japonica x Hedera helix)   Zone 8
(Botanical Wonder)

541   Evergreen. A botanical hybrid between Aralia (Fatsia) and Hedera (Ivy). Has leaves of the Aralia. Grows as a small heavy vine or mounded shrub and is excellent espalliered against a wall. Grows in heavy shade, partial shade or full sun.   Planting Group 1 or 4

Ficus repens (F. pumila)   Zone 9
(Creeping Fig)

542   Evergreen. One of the few vines that will cling to a masonry wall. Quite vigorous once it starts to climb so wedge it against the wall when planting. Also used indoors as a hanging pot plant.
Planting Group 1

Gelsemium sempervirens   Zone 7
(Carolina Jessamine)

543   Evergreen. Beautiful vine with long, tubular, yellow flowers. These are borne in great abundance from January to April. Best in the warmer regions and in full sun.   Planting Group 1

Hedera canariensis   Zone 8
(Algerian Ivy)

544   Widely used as a bank cover in California and also as a climbing vine to cover a fence. The leaves are large, up to five inches and are more tolerant of hot sun than those of most varieties of Ivy. A variegated form is also available.   Planting Group 1

545 *Hedera helix*

546 *Hedera helix* 'Hahnsii'

Hedera helix   Zone 4

(English Ivy)

545 One of the hardiest and most widely used of the Ivies. Usually used as a ground cover for banks or as a substitute for a lawn grown throughout the United States.   Planting Group 1

Hedera helix 'Hahnsii'   Zone 6

(Hahn's Ivy)

546 Very low growing variety with small, light green leaves and dense branching growth. Particularly suited for areas where only a three or four inch deep cover is wanted. Sun or part shade.
                                    Planting Group 1 or 4

547 *Hibbertia volubilis*

Hibbertia volubilis   Zone 9

(Guinea Gold Vine)

547 Excellent evergreen vine to ten feet and especially happy in coastal areas. Shiny dark green leaves and bright yellow two and one-half inch single flowers. Best in partial shade. Planting Group 4

Jasminum magnificum (J. nitidum)   Zone 10

(Angel Wing Jasmine)

548 A climbing evergreen shrub or semi-vine with large evergreen foliage and glistening, fragrant, white, windmill-like flowers in summer.   Planting Group 1

548 *Jasminum magnificum*

549 *Jasminum polyanthum*

552 *Lonicera japonica* 'Halliana'

550 *Jasminum primulinum*

551 *Lonicera hildebrandiana*

Jasminun polyanthum   Zone 8

(Pink Jasmine)

549 A vigorous evergreen climber with lacy evergreen foliage. Starting in April it produces masses of pink buds in nice clusters that open to white flowers. Grows in any soil. Fragrant.

Planting Group 1

Jasminum primulinum (J. mesnyi)   Zone 8

(Primrose Jasmine)

550 Evergreen. Fast growing vine to ten or fifteen feet with bright green leaves and lemon yellow flowers. Excellent bank cover if you have the room. Planted at six foot centers, this plant will grow to five or six feet then cascade over, making one solid mass of bright green foliage and covered all spring with double yellow flowers.

Planting Group 1

Lonicera hildebrandiana   Zone 9

(Giant Burmese Honeysuckle)

551 A fast growing evergreen vine with large shiny leaves and clusters of giant, six inch cream and yellow fragrant flowers, blooming for more than six months, commencing in late spring. Planting Group 1

Lonicera japonica 'Halliana'   Zone 5

(Hall's Japanese Honeysuckle or Common Honeysuckle)
552 This vigorous evergreen vine grows in any soil and is used both as a ground cover and a fence cover. Intensely fragrant, white flowers changing to yellow.   Planting Group 1.

Mandevilla suaveolens 'Alice DuPont'   Zone 9

(Chile Jasmine)

553   Evergreen. Fast growing to ten to fifteen feet. Dark green leaves to three inches with clusters of wide trumpet-like, intensely fragrant pink flowers. It grows in the sun in rich soil and needs ample water.
Planting Group 1

554   *Passiflora jamesonii*

553   *Mandevilla suaveolens* 'Alice DuPont'

Passiflora jamesonii   Zone 9

(Jameson or Pink Passion Vine)

554   Evergreen vine with glossy, dark green leaves. It is fast growing and an excellent fence or bank cover. A profuse bloomer all summer with four inch tubular flowers that are a lovely coral pink color.
Planting Group 1

555   *Passiflora pfordtii*

Passiflora pfordtii (P. alato-caerulea)   Zone 9

(Passion Vine)

555   Large exotic flowers on this fast growing evergreen vine. The fragrant flowers are three to four inches across with white petals touched with blue and lavender and a center crown of purple. Flowers all summer.
Planting Group 1

Polygonum aubertii   Zone 4

(Silver Lace Vine)

556   Evergreen to fifteen or twenty degrees, then deciduous. Used for a very quick growing shade or cover. Likes a rich well drained soil. Produces masses of fragrant flowers from late spring until fall.
Planting Group 1

556   *Polygonum aubertii*

557 *Rhynchospermum jasminoides*

560 *Solanum jasminoides*

558 *Rosa banksiae* 'Lutea'

559 *Solandra guttata*

Rhynchospermum jasminoides (Trachelospermum jasminoides)
Zone 7

(Star Jasmine)

557 Evergreen. One of the finest vines for the shade but will do equally well in full sun. Fragrant white flowers in June and July. It is grown as a vine or a mounded shrub and is one of the most beautiful ground covers, but not for a dry bank. This plant likes a peat moss or leaf mold soil with moist roots at all times.

Planting Group 1 or 4

Rosa banksiae 'Lutea'
Zone 6

(Yellow Banksia Rose)

558 Lovely miniature double yellow flowers (the size of a good thick button), borne in clusters on this shiny bright evergreen. Few thorns, if any and it needs little maintenance. Makes an excellent espalier in the full sun. (Rosa Banksiae Alba also available. Same characteristics except white in color.)

Planting Group 1

Solandra guttata
Zone 9

(Cup of Gold Vine)

559 Evergreen, woody vine up to twenty-five feet. Large, broad, six inch leaves, with fragrant, yellow trumpet flowers having brown stripes. They are fully eight inches long and four inches across. It is one of the fastest growing of all vines. Is salt tolerant at the seashore. Requires full sun.

Planting Group 1

Solanum jasminoides
Zone 9

(Potato Vine)

560 Evergreen to about twenty-eight degrees, then deciduous. Fast growing to about fifteen feet, with small bright green foliage and white, star-shaped flowers tinged with blue. Needs severe cutting every winter. Sun or partial shade.

Planting Group 1

561   Solanum rantonnetti

562   Stephanotis floribunda

Solanum rantonnetti   Zone 10
(Blue Solanum or Paraguay Night Shade)

561   Medium to large evergreen vine or shrub. Deep blue flowers
from early spring throughout the summer. Must be pruned severely
to keep it neat.   Planting Group 1

Stephanotis floribunda   Zone 10
(Madagascar Jasmine)

562   An evergreen vine grown outdoors only in the warmest areas
of California but elsewhere as an indoor outdoor plant. Very fragrant
waxy, funnel-shaped, white flowers. Frequently used in bridal bou-
quets. When used outdoors, grow in filtered sun with shaded roots.
                                        Planting Group 3

563   Tecoma capensis

Tecoma capensis (Tecomaria capensis)   Zone 9
(Cape Honeysuckle)

563   Evergreen. A vine or stiff shrub to fifteen feet with shiny, dark
green foliage and clusters of orange-red, trumpet-shaped flowers. Full
sun in well-drained soil. Excellent at the seashore. Planting Group 1

Wisteria venusta   Zone 5
(Silky Wisteria)

568   Deciduous. Leaves have silky hairs. Individual flowers are very
large that open all at once making a heavy cluster of flowers. Varieties
are W. Alba and W. Violacea, a fragrant double purple-blue double.
                                        Planting Group 1

568   Wisteria venusta

WISTERIA

All are deciduous woody vines. Flowers borne in the spring before the leaves. They thrive in deep rich soil. For ample flowering, fertilize and have even moisture during the summer. Needed pruning should be done in the fall.

Wisteria floribunda longissima 'Alba'
> (Japanese wisteria)
> Pure white flowers from two to four feet long.

Wisteria floribunda longissima 'Rosea'
> Light pink flowers two to three feet long.

Wisteria floribunda longissima 'Royal Purple'
> Eighteen inches to two feet. Purple blooms.

Wisteria floribunda longissima 'Geisha'
> Moderate length blooms and the bluest of this group.

All Planting Group 1

564   *Wisteria floribunda longissima* 'Alba'

565   *Wisteria floribunda longissima* 'Rosea'

566   *Wisteria floribunda longissima* 'Royal Purple'

567   *Wisteria sinensis*

Wisteria sinensis (Wisteria chinensis)   Zone 5
(Chinese Wisteria)

567   Deciduous. Most cutting grown plants in western nurseries are of this type. Flower clusters are about twelve inches and slightly fragrant. Will bloom in considerable shade. Varieties are violet-blue (and usually called purple by nurserymen) and alba. Slightly fragrant.
                                          Planting Group 1

CONIFERS

Abies balsamea 'Nana'   Zone 3

(Dwarf Balsam Fir)

569   A very slow growing, dense, dark green mound, seldom more than eighteen inches tall. An interesting bonsai plant for the rock garden in partial shade. Does not like to dry out. Planting Group 1

Abies concolor   Zone 3

(White Fir)

570   A native West Coast conifer greatly valued as a Christmas tree and widely grown in Western gardens. Makes a very symmetrical tree and it stands pruning. Needles are about an inch to inch and a half long and bluish green in color. Usually a ten foot tree in ten years but eventually over one hundred feet.   Planting Group 1

570   Abies concolor

Abies lasiocarpa   Zone 4

(Alpine Fir)

571   Specimens usually two to four feet are collected high in the Cascade mountains, where storms twist them into contorted forms to make them artistic tub plants. Very slow growing. Found mostly in Northwest nurseries.   Planting Group 1

569   Abies balsamea 'Nana'

571   Abies lasiocarpa

572   Abies pinsapo 'Glauca'

573   Araucaria araucana

Abies pinsapo 'Glauca'   Zone 5
(Blue Spanish Fir)

572   A fine tree with short, stiff, deep bluish-green foliage and dense symmetrical growth. A native of Spain which will grow in the warm dry areas to forty feet. Scarce in the trade.   Planting Group 1

Araucaria araucana (A. imbricata)   Zone 7
(Monkey Puzzle Tree)

573   This interesting tree has hard, green, stiff, prickly leaves on heavy spreading branches. This tree, formal in shape, grows rapidly for the first ten years, but then slows down as the tree fills out. A hundred foot tree in its native land but seldom over fifty feet on the West Coast.   Planting Group 1

Araucaria bidwillii   Zone 8
(Bunyabunya)

574   Bold symmetrical tree to sixty feet with down-curving limbs covered with sharply pointed, green leaves.   Planting Group 1

574   Araucaria bidwillii

575   Araucaria excelsa

578   Cedrus atlantica 'Glauca Pendula'

Araucaria excelsa (A. Heterophylla)   Zone 8
(Norfolk Island or Star Pine)

575   Very formal tree usually grown indoors until it gets too big,
then planted in the garden where it grows into a beautiful symmetrical
tree to over forty feet.   Planting Group 1

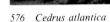

576   Cedrus atlantica

Cedrus atlantica   Zone 6
(Atlas Cedar)

576   Large pyramidal tree with attractive blue-green needle-like foliage. Can be used as an excellent bonsai specimen if started early
and kept in a tub. This tree will grow to twenty feet in fifteen years
and eventually to eighty feet.   Planting Group 1

Cedrus atlantica 'Glauca'   Zone 6
(Blue Atlas Cedar)

577   Grafted plants insure the bright blue foliage of this plant that
is considered the most beautiful of the blue conifers. Grows in a natural
bonsai style.   Planting Group 1

Cedrus atlantica 'Glauca Pendula'   Zone 6
578   This beautiful weeping form of C.A. Glauca can be trained to
any shape. The branches droop vertically and with age makes a superb
specimen. Crawls along the ground unless staked. Planting Group 1

577   Cedrus atlantica 'Glauca'

579   *Cedrus deodara*

Cedrus deodara   Zone 7

(California Christmas Tree)

579   Rich silver gray-green on this fast growing
tree that has wide spreading branches and
needle-like leaves and drooping tip. It is best
in the interior valley where it grows to one
hundred feet or more but not too good along
the coast.   Planting Group 1

581   *Cedrus deodara* 'Prostrata'

Cedrus deodara 'Aurea'   Zone 7

580   This grafted plant is not as fast growing nor does this variety
grow as big as C. Deodara. This variety has golden yellow foliage
turning to yellowish-green in the fall. Seldom more than twenty
feet.   Planting Group 1

Cedrus deodara 'Prostrata'   Zone 7

(Weeping Deodar)

581   This variety will grow flat on the ground or even hang over
a wall. Stands pruning. Very scarce in the trade.   Planting Group 1

Cedrus libani   Zone 5

(Cedar of Lebanon)

582   Large evergreen to one hundred feet with short blue-green
needles. Each tree will vary in shape and foliage color. Train to desired
shape. Slow growing. Scarce in the trade.   Planting Group 1

580   *Cedrus deodara* 'Aurea'

582   *Cedrus libani*

583   *Chamaecyparis lawsoniana*

584   *Chamaecyparis lawsoniana* 'Allumii'

Chamaecyparis lawsoniana   Zone 5
(Port Orford Cedar or Lawson Cypress)

583   Important timber tree in coastal Oregon and Northern California. It grows in a pyramidal form to one hundred feet or more. Many varieties in the trade today trace their origin to this variety.
Planting Group 1

Chamaecyparis lawsoniana 'Allumii'   Zone 5
(Blue Lawson Cypress)

584   Compact, narrow, pyramidal tree to thirty feet with flat metallic-blue foliage. Best in the interior where the drainage is good with only limited amounts of water.   Planting Group 2

Chamaecyparis lawsoniana 'Nidiformis'   Zone 6
(Birdnest Cypress)

586   The natural habit of this plant is wider than tall; seldom reaching a height of more than four feet. An excellent, dark green, low growing foundation plant for a hot sunny location. Needs good drainage.
Planting Group 2

Chamaecyparis lawsoniana 'Ellwoodii'   Zone 5
(Ellwood Cypress)

585   A moderate to slow grower of columnar type to ten feet. Foliage is silver-blue, soft and lacy. It is neat and attractive but must be planted where the drainage is excellent as it, like most cypresses, is extremely sensitive to wet feet.   Planting Group 2

586   *Chamaecyparis lawsoniana* 'Nidiformis'

585   *Chamaecyparis lawsoniana* 'Ellwoodii'

588   *Chamaecyparis obtusa* 'Aurea'

587   *Chamaecyparis obtusa*

Chamaecyparis obtusa   Zone 5
(Hinoki Cypress)

587   This most artistic tree is slow growing and most gardeners treat it as a dwarf even though it will grow to a small tree up to fifteen and even fifty feet in fifty years. Generally pyramidal in habit, it is best when trained to emphasize its irregular branching. Needs good drainage and is best in the Northern California, Oregon, and Washington coastal areas in full sun and is not too happy in the hot interior.   Planting Group 2

Chamaecyparis obtusa 'Aurea'   Zone 6
(Golden Hinoki)

588   Similar to C. Obtusa, but slower growing. Even in the cooler coastal regions, this plant is best with morning sun only, as the foliage burns rather easily. Needs good drainage.
                         Planting Group 2

Chamaecyparis obtusa 'Crippsii'   Zone 6
(Crippsi Cypress)

589   Pyramidal in form, but a more open habit of growth than most Chamaecyparis Obtusas. One of the most beautiful specimen trees we have in the fifteen or twenty foot range. Best in the cooler coastal areas of Northern California and farther North.   Planting Group 2

589   *Chamaecyparis obtusa* 'Crippsii'

590   *Chamaecyparis obtusa* 'Minima'

593   *Chamaecyparis pisifera* 'Cyano Viridis'

591   *Chamaecyparis obtusa* 'Nana'

Chamaecyparis obtusa 'Minima'   Zone 7

590   A soft textured, compact, globular plant seldom more than a foot tall but up to three feet broad. Excellent rock garden or pot plant.   Planting Group 1

Chamaecyparis obtusa 'Nana'   Zone 5
(Dwarf Hinoki Cypress)

591   Low, globular plant with deep green foliage. It is rated as one of the choicest plants in the garden. Excellent tub plant; very slow growing and needs good drainage. It must be protected from dogs. Best in the cooler coastal regions.   Planting Group 2

Chamaecyparis obtusa 'Torulosa'   Zone 5

592   This plant is different. Dark green twisted, threadlike branches with scalelike leaves which give this plant a natural bonsai look. It will grow to six feet but with a little bonsai pruning, it is easily kept to three feet. Excellent pot or rock garden plant.   Planting Group 2

Chamaecyparis pisifera 'Cyano Viridis'   Zone 4
(Blue Plume Cypress)

593   A graceful pyramidal tree to ten feet, sometimes more, with soft plumelike, silvery-blue foliage that forms an irregular rounded cone-shaped tree. One of the few "blue" plants that will tolerate the shade.   Planting Group 4

592   *Chamaecyparis obtusa* 'Torulosa'

595   *Chamaecyparis pisifera* 'Plumosa'

Chamaecyparis pisifera 'Plumosa' Zone 5
(Plume Cypress)

595   A very nice, conical, small tree with dark
green foliage and short needles. While this tree
will eventually grow to twenty feet, it is quite
slow to eight or ten feet and is a good small,
garden evergreen.   Planting Group 2

596   *Cryptomeria japonica* 'Elegans'

594   *Chamaecyparis pisifera* 'Filifera' and *C.p.* 'Filifera Aurea'

Chamaecyparis pisifera 'Filifera'   Zone 3
(Threadbranch Cypress)

594   While this plant will eventually make a small tree, it is usually
planted as a large shrub, and with minimum amounts of pruning
can be kept within bounds. If thinned, it has an oriental look that
is hard to beat.   Planting Group 2

Chamaecyparis pisifera 'Filifera Aurea'   Zone 3
(Golden Threadleaf Cypress)

594   This slightly golden threadleaf variety is not so upright as the
green form. The branches are flattened, threadleaf, and slightly drooping. Very attractive.   Planting Group 2

Cyptomeria japonica 'Elegans'   Zone 5
(Plume Cryptomeria)

596   Feathery, gray-green, soft textured foliage that turns purplish
or coppery-red in winter. An outstanding pyramid to twenty-five feet
or more.   Planting Group 1

Cryptomeria japonica 'Elegans Nana'   Zone 6
597   A compact pyramidal dwarf form with bright foliage turning
to plum red in the fall.   Planting Group 4

597   *Cryptomeria japonica* 'Elegans Nana'

598   Cupressocyparis leylandii

Cupressocyparis leylandii   Zone 5
(Leyland Cypress)

598   A rapid growing narrow pyramid to thirty feet with striking green, dense foliage. Excellent tall hedge plant or windbreak. Needs pruning when young and accepts a wide variety of soils and climates.   Planting Group 1

599   Cupressus glabra

Cupressus macrocarpa   Zone 7
(Monterey Cypress)

600   A good seashore plant. Beautiful dark green tree to forty feet becoming picturesquely irregular when exposed to wind or sea. Often used as a seashore windbreak or tall hedge.   Planting Group 1

Cupressus glabra (C. arizonica)   Zone 6
(Arizona Cypress)

599   A tall upright conifer to twenty feet with grayish-green foliage. Its ability to stand heat and drought in the southwest makes this tree a favorite in hot weather country.
                    Planting Goup 1

Cupressus sempervirens 'Glauca'   Zone 7
(Italian Cypress)

601   Narrow, dense columnar tree with silvery-blue-green foliage. Often twenty feet tall and only two feet in diameter. A fine accent plant for the landscape.   Planting Group 1

601   Cupressus sempervirens 'Glauca'

600   Cupressus macrocarpa

602   Juniperus chinensis 'Armstrongii'

603   Juniperus chinensis 'Armstrongii Coasti'

604   Juniperus chinensis 'Blaauwii'

605   Juniperus chinensis 'Blue Point'

Juniperus chinensis 'Armstrongii'   Zone 4
(Armstrong Juniper)

602   Lacy, light green foliage on this compact, medium-size, nestlike Juniper. Its closely knit habit of growth makes this an excellent garden addition.   Planting Group 1

Juniperus chinensis 'Armstrongii Coasti'   Zone 4
(Coasti Juniper)

603   Outstanding golden coloring on this dense compact plant. Very little trimming is necessary and the gold holds even in cold weather. Very similar to J.C.A. "Old Gold"   Planting Group 1

Juniperus chinensis 'Blaauwii'   Zone 5
(Blaauw's Juniper)

604   An upright vase shaped Juniper to about four feet with dark blue foliage on this neat, compact plant.   Planting Group 1

Juniperus chinensis 'Blue Point'   Zone 5
(Blue Point Juniper)

605   A very formal appearance and dense pyramidal form, and beautiful blue-gray foliage make this a very excellent plant. Also sought after because of its tolerance to extremes of heat and to poor soil.
                                                        Planting Group 1

606   Juniperus chinensis 'Hetzii Glauca'

607   Juniperus chinensis 'Pfitzeriana'

Juniperus chinensis 'Hetzii Glauca'   Zone 3
(Hetzii Glauca Juniper)

606   Semi-erect Juniper with a light frosty blue foliage. It is fast
growing with a medium large spread.   Planting Group 1

Juniperus chinensis 'Pfitzeriana'   Zone 3
(Pfitzer Juniper)

607   A fast growing, spreading shrub with rich gray-green, feathery
foliage. Grows three to four feet high and six to eight feet across.
Can be kept in bounds by heavy pruning. Used as a low accent plant
or as a ground cover.   Planting Group 1

608   Juniperus chinensis 'Pfitzeriana Aurea'

Juniperus chinensis 'Pfitzeriana Aurea'   Zone 4
(Golden Tip Juniper)

608   Beautiful gray-greenish foliage tipped with gold throughout the
year. Grows to four or five feet tall and about eight feet across.
          Planting Group 1

Juniperus chinensis 'Pfitzeriana Glauca'   Zone 4
(Blue Pfitzer)

609   Soft silver-blue foliage and a spreading compact habit of growth.
Mature plants may reach six to eight feet in height with a ten to
fifteen foot spread.   Planting Group 1

609   Juniperus chinensis 'Pfitzeriana Glauca'

610 *Junipers chinensis* 'Procumbens'

611   *Juniperus chinensis* 'Procumbens Nana'

612   *Juniperus chinensis* 'Robusta Green'

613   *Juniperus chinensis* 'San Jose'

Juniperus chinensis procumbens   Zone 4
(Japanese Garden Juniper)

610   A very flat, wide-spreading (to six feet) variety with sharply
pointed bluish-green foliage. Excellent around rock work and widely
used by Japanese in their gardens.   Planting Group 1

Juniperus chinensis procumbens 'Nana'   Zone 4
611   Extremely compact, low-spreading Juniper with dense, blue-
green foliage. Excellent bonsai material. One of the best of the low
creeping varieties of the low-creeping evergreens. Spectacular when
grown "staked" in a container and shaped.   Planting Group 1

Juniperus chinensis 'Robusta Green'   Zone 5
612   Informal, irregular upright growth with bright green foliage. A
most outstanding Juniper but fairly slow growing. Planting Group 1

Juniperus chinensis 'San Jose'   Zone 4
(San Jose Juniper)

613   An excellent semi-prostrate Juniper with sage-green compact
foliage. One of the best Junipers for bonsai use. Good tub Juniper.
                                                      Planting Group 1

615   *Juniperus chinensis* 'Torulosa'

Juniperus chinensis 'Sea Green'   Zone 5
(Sea Green Juniper)

614   An outstanding spreading Juniper with deep green coloring. It has a compact habit and arching branches. Very similar growth to J. Pfitzer, but does not grow so fast, but will grow taller.   Planting Group 1

614   *Juniperus chinensis* 'Sea Green'

Juniperus chinensis 'Torulosa'   Zone 5
(Hollywood Juniper)

615   Artistic dense upright growing Juniper. Twisted branches and rich dark green foliage. Should be planted away from the house where it has enough room to twist and turn, performing the way it should.   Planting Group 1

Juniperus communis stricta   Zone 4
(Irish Juniper)

616   Fast growing. Very narrow column with gray-green foliage. Many similar plants are sold under the following names such as J.C. **Fastigiata and J.C. Hibernica**   Planting Group 1

Juniperus conferta 'Blue Pacific'   Zone 6
(Shore Juniper)

617   Improved form of J. Conferta. A low-creeping form, seldom over six inches tall. Excellent around rock work or hanging over a wall. Best in the cooler coastal areas as this one does not like full sun in the hot interior.   Planting Group 1

617   *Juniperus conferta* 'Blue Pacific'

616   *Juniperus communis* 'Stricta'

618   *Juniperus horizontalis* 'Bar Harbor'

Juniperus horizontalis 'Bar Harbor'   Zone 4
(Bar Harbor Juniper)

618   One of the best of the very prostrate Junipers because as it grows, its branches hug the ground. Summer foliage is soft gray-blue turning to silvery plum color in winter.   Planting Group 1

619   *Juniperus horizontalis*

620   *Juniperus horizontalis* 'Variegata'

Juniperus horizontalis (J. prostrata)   Zone 4

619   Prostrate, creeping to form a low, flat compact mat with stiff bluish-green foliage that make interesting patterns.
          Planting Group 1

621   *Juniperus horizontalis* 'Wiltoni'

Juniperus horizontalis 'Variegata' *(J. prostrata variegata)*
          Zone 4

620   This low growing, flat spreading Juniper has bluish-green foliage liberally splashed with blotches of creamy variegation. Variegation will burn in very hot sun.   Planting Group 1

Juniperus horizontalis 'Wiltoni'   Zone 4
(Wilton Carpet Juniper)

621   This living carpet is similar in habit to Bar Harbor and one of the finest low trailing Junipers. Foliage is intense silver-blue.
          Planting Group 1

Juniperus sabina 'Arcadia'   Zone 3
(Arcadia Juniper)

622   Bright green foliage with a lacy texture on this attractive, low growing evergreen. Fine mass border or foundation plant.
          Planting Group 1

Juniperus sabina 'Broadmoor'   Zone 3

623   A fairly new introduction with attractive green foliage. Grows to about one foot. Will take full sun but is also happy with coastal conditions.   Planting Group 1

622 *Juniperus sabina* 'Arcadia'

623 *Juniperus sabina* 'Broadmoor'

Juniperus sabina 'Buffalo'　　　　Zone 3

624 A new bright green, wide spreading, low growing form of Juniper with soft feathery branches. Very hardy and excellent in coastal areas as well as colder areas.　　　Planting Group 1

Juniperus sabina 'Tamariscifolia'　　Zone 3

(Tamarix Juniper or Tam Juniper)

625 Spreads close to the ground, making a solid mat, seldom over eighteen inches in mature plants. Foliage is bright blue-green. Excellent ground cover.　　　Planting Group 1

624 *Juniperus sabina* 'Buffalo'

Juniperus scopulorum 'Blue Haven'　　Zone 4

(Blue Haven Juniper)

626 A very compact pyramidal form to about twelve feet. It is one of the bluest of all the Junipers and makes an excellent accent plant where color contrast is needed. Needs full sun.　　Planting Group 1

626 *Juniperus scopulorum* 'Blue Haven'

625 *Juniperus sabina* 'Tamariscifolia'

627 Juniperus scopulorum 'Pathfinder'

628   Juniperus squamata 'Meyeri'

Juniperus squamata 'Meyeri'   Zone 5
(Meyer Juniper)

628   This is an oddly shaped, blue-green, rather stiff Juniper which grows to six or eight feet tall with about the same spread.
Planting Group 1

Juniperus scopulorum 'Pathfinder'
Zone 3
(Pathfinder Juniper)

627   A showy, dense, broad pyramidal Juniper with a bright blue-gray cast to the foliage. Full sun and a dry location.   Planting Group 1

Juniperus virginana prostrata 'Silver Spreader'   Zone 4
(Silver Spreader Juniper)

629   A very delightful spreading conifer with shiny silvery foliage. Excellent ground cover.   Planting Group 1

Libocedrus decurrens (Calocedrus decurrens)   Zone 5
(Incense Cedar)

630   A very symmetrical, narrow columnar tree to one hundred feet with deep green, fragrant foliage. A California native.
Planting Group 1

630   Libocedrus decurrens

629   Juniperus virginana prostrata 'Silver Spreader'

633 *Picea excelsa* 'Nidiformis'

Metasequoia glyptostroboides   Zone 5
(Dawn Redwood)

631 Deciduous. A beautiful, rapid growing conifer, resembling the California coastal Redwood. The foliage is bright green and very soft to the touch. Grows best in soil with lots of humus and generous amounts of water.   Planting Group 1

631 *Metasequoia glyptostroboides*

Picea excelsa 'Nidiformis'   Zone 4
(Nest Spruce)

633 Low, rounded nestlike shrub that grows two to four inches a year to about eighteen inches, and five to six feet across. Needles are very short and fine. New foliage bright green. Best in cooler areas.   Planting Group 1

Picea excelsa (P. abies)   Zone 2
(Norway Spruce)

632 Widely sold as a living Christmas tree. This tree does quite well in cooler areas. Needs pruning to keep it compact. Planting Goup 1

Picea excelsa 'Pendula'   Zone 3
(Weeping Norway Spruce)

634 The dense, rich green foliage on the branches and branchlets of this interesting specimen makes it a favorite. A natural bonsai type plant that grows best in Northern California along the coast and in the Northwest.   Planting Group 1

634 *Picea excelsa* 'Pendula'

632 *Picea excelsa*

635   *Picea excelsa* 'Pygmaea'

637   *Picea pungens*

Picea excelsa 'Pygmaea'   Zone 6

635   Stiff, deep green attractive needles on this
very slow growing evergreen conifer. In twenty
years this one could be only two to three feet
tall and two feet broad. For a rock garden or
a tub plant this one is excellent. Needs well
drained, moist soil.   Planting Group 1

Picea glauca 'Conica'   Zone 3
(Alberta Spruce)

636   A miniature tree that maintains a perfect conical shape and grows
only about six inches a year with very short needles, bright green
when new, then gray-green. Excellent tub plant and miniature Christmas tree for years.   Planting Group 1

Picea pungens   Zone 3
(Colorado Spruce)

637   A broad pyramidal Spruce with horizontal and stiff sharp green
needle foliage. All are seedling grown and usually fifty percent will
be green; thirty-five percent blue-green and fifteen percent blue. The
blue and blue-green command a premium price.   Planting Group 2

Picea pungens 'Kosteriana'   Zone 3
(Koster Blue Spruce)

638   Grafted plants only. These have a richer blue form and longer
needles. Very erratic grower in early stages. Shaping will help attain
"Christmas tree" look.   Planting Group 2

636   *Picea glauca* 'Conica'

638   *Picea pungens* 'Kosteriana'

641   *Pinus canariensis*

Picea pungens 'Moerheimii'   Zone 3

(Moerhiemi Spruce)

639   Grafts only. Similar to the Koster variety but more compact and grows straighter.   Planting Group 2

Pinus aristata   Zone 1

(Bristlecone Pine)

640   A beautiful, extremely hardy conifer. Will stand temperatures from one hundred degrees above to fifty degrees below zero. Very slow growing artistic tub plant or bonsai for a long period of time. Good drainage necessary.   Planting Group 1

Pinus canariensis   Zone 8

(Canary Island Pine)

641   One of the most beautiful pines grown in warmer climates. While considered an "ugly duckling" in a container, it grows to a hundred foot straight, symmetrical tree with horizontal branches evenly spaced in whorls. The long needles are thickly placed in large tufts. Somewhat tender in the colder areas.   Planting Group 1

639   *Picea pungens* 'Moerheimii'

Pinus densiflora 'Umbraculifera' Zone 4

(Table Mountain Pine or Tanyosho Pine)

642   Excellent container or rock garden plant usually growing wider than it does tall. Grafted plants only. It can take twenty years to get to be six feet tall and as wide. Planting Group 1

642   *Pinus densiflora* 'Umbraculifera'

640   *Pinus aristata*

643   Pinus halepensis

Pinus halepensis   Zone 7
(Aleppo Pine)

643   A round-headed, irregularly shaped pine
to forty feet with short, gray-green needles. This
pine thrives on neglect and is best when planted
in a very dry location. Also good near the seashore.   Planting Group 1

644   Pinus mugo mughus

Pinus mugo mughus   Zone 2
(Mugho Pine)

644   One of the smallest of all the pines in the trade, growing about
as wide as it does tall. Widely used in rock gardens; also an excellent
low foundation or container plant. Very slow grower; likes a dry
location best. Stands pruning.   Planting Group 1

Pinus nigra   Zone 3
(Austrian Black Pine)

645   A large densely-foliaged pyramid pine with dark shiny foliage.
Grows to about forty feet.   Planting Group 1

Pinus patula   Zone 8
(Jelecote or Mexican Yellow Pine)

646   A very graceful and unusual pine growing to about forty feet.
A beautiful, irregular tree with long yellow-green silky needles that
hang down giving it a "different" look with its lacy appearance.
                                                 Planting Group 2

645   Pinus nigra

646   Pinus patula

647   *Pinus pinea*

648   *Pinus radiata*

Pinus pinea   Zone 7

(Italian Stone Pine)

647   Native to the Mediterranean where it will stand heat and drought, but is not hurt by generous garden watering. Never attractive as a nursery size tree, but after ten years its picturesque spreading beauty is evident and greatly enjoyed.   Planting Group 1

Pinus sylvestris   Zone 4

(Scotch Pine)

650   When young, this pine is straight, well-branched and pyramidal, but as it grows it becomes irregular and picturesque. Grows to eighty feet. Good almost anywhere from coast to coast except in the desert.

Planting Group 1

Pinus radiata   Zone 8

(Monterey Pine)

648   A widely planted pine tree around the world. Grows rapidly and succeeds anywhere. Used as a windbreak or an individual specimen. Deep green foliage and a tall symmetrical tree to twenty feet in ten years, and seventy-five feet or more eventually.

Planting Group 1

Pinus strobus 'Nana'   Zone 4

649   This five-needle pine is the dwarf form of P. Strobus that is native to Northwestern United States. It has very soft foliage and a nice rounded shape. However, it does not like to dry out and does not like the wind. Excellent rock garden or tub plant. Found mostly in Northwest nurseries.   Planting Group 1

649   *Pinus strobus* 'Nana'

650   *Pinus sylvestris*

651   Pinus sylvestris 'Fastigiata'

654   Podocarpus gracilior

652   Pinus thunbergii

Pinus sylvestris 'Fastigiata'   Zone 4

651   Similar foliage and growing conditions as the parent but the branches of this cultivar grow straight and next to the trunk. When the tree is ten feet tall it is seldom more than three feet in diameter.   Planting Group 1

Pinus thunbergii   Zone 5
(Japanese Black Pine)

652-653   Irregular pattern of pyramidal growth, blackish-gray bark and sharp green needles. Decorative in planters when young and kept pruned and shaped. Two pictures have been used, one trained as a bonsai, the other allowed to grow. Both are about the same age.
                                                         Planting Group 1

653   Pinus thunbergii

655   Podocarpus macrophyllus

656   *Podocarpus macrophyllus* 'Maki'

657   *Pseudotsuga taxifolia*

Podocarpus gracilior   Zone 9
(Fern Pine)

654   A plant of compact growth similar to P. Elongatus, but this has a heavier trunk and does not drop its lower branches. The foliage is much denser. Excellent tub plant both indoors and outdoors and in the garden used as a heavy-trimmed shrub, a small tree or espalier. Few people realize this group of plants are conifers.
Planting Group 1

Podocarpus macrophyllus   Zone 7
(Yew Podocarpus)

655   Evergreen shrub or small tree to fifteen feet with Yew-like deep rich green foliage. Usually kept trimmed like a Yew to a columnar form. Excellent indoor plant.   Planting Group 1 or 4

Podocarpus macrophyllus 'Maki'   Zone 7
(Shrubby Yew)

656   Similar to P. Macrophyllus but the plant is more compact, more erect and the needles are much shorter. Likes to be pruned to shape.   Planting Group 1 or 4

Sciadopitys verticillata   Zone 4
(Umbrella Pine)

658   Evergreen conifer to about twenty-five feet on the West coast, but to one hundred feet in native Japan. Young plants are symmetrical and rather narrow. The dark green needles are three to six inches long and in whorls. The plants should never be allowed to dry out and require a rich, well-drained soil. Excellent tub specimen or in the ground. Can take full sun (or shade) near the coast, requires a rich, well-drained soil and should have afternoon shade in the hot interior.   Planting Group 2

Pseudotsuga taxifolia   Zone 5
(P. menziesii)
(Douglas Fir)

657   Native to the Pacific Coast from California north and much prized as a Christmas tree. Sharply pyramidal form when young growing eventually to two hundred feet. soft, fragrant foliage.   Planting Group 1

658   *Sciadopitys verticillata*

659   *Sequoia gigantea*

660   *Sequoia gigantea* 'Pendula'

Sequoia gigantea (Sequoiadendron giganteum)   Zone 6
(California Big Tree)

659   The giant Redwood has a conical shape with a dense branching
habit and blue-green foliage. It grows too fast and is usually too big
for the average garden.   Planting Group 1

Sequoia sempervirens   Zone 7
(Coast Redwood)

661   A fast growing conical tree, with dark green flat needle-like
leaves, usually too big for a city garden. Best with regular watering.
                                                            Planting Group 1

Sequoia gigantea 'Pendula' *(Sequoiadendron)*   Zone 6
660   A weeping form of the giant "Big Tree" and for the first few
years seldom has branches over two feet long. It has a very interesting
shape and is very scarce in the trade, mostly in the Northwest. Must
be placed carefully in the garden for best display. Planting Group 1

661   *Sequoia sempervirens*

662   *Taxus baccata*

666   *Taxus baccata* 'Repandens Aurea'

Taxus baccata   Zone 6
(English Yew)

662   As gardens become smaller and smaller, this tree is fast decreasing in popularity as it needs a great deal of room. It is listed in this book only because so many people ask for it by the common name in nurseries when they are talking about tight, upright pyramidal form, Taxus Baccata Fastigiata. Taxus Baccata, the English Yew, spreads as wide as it grows tall, up to thirty feet.   Planting Group 2

Taxus Baccata 'Fastigiata'   Zone 6
(Irish Yew)

663   Formal slender column of the deepest green foliage. Ideal accent plant beside doors or in a corner. Slow upright growth. Will not stand poorly drained soil.   Planting Group 2

Taxus baccata 'Fastigiata aurea'   Zone 6
664   Same as above except with golden tips and margins.
                                                  Planting Group 1

Taxus baccata 'Repandens'   Zone 5
(Spreading English Yew)

665   A very useful spreading plant, seldom more than two feet tall, ideal for foundation planting as well as hanging over a wall.
                                                  Planting Group 2

663   *Taxus baccata* 'Fastigiata'

Taxus baccata   Zone 6
'Repandens aurea'
(Golden Spreading Yew)

666   Long golden branches seldom more than two feet tall but spreading a great deal more. Excellent rock garden or low foundation plant but needs good drainage.   Planting Group 2

664   *Taxus baccata* 'Fastigiata Aurea'

665   *Taxus baccata* 'Repandens'

668   *Thuja occidentalis* 'Pyramidalis'

Thuja occidentalis 'Little Gem'   Zone 2
(Green Globe Arborvitae)

667   Dark green foliage with short, dense,
green growth to about three feet. Very slow.
                                    Planting Group 1

670   *Thuja orientalis* 'Aurea Nana'

667   *Thuja occidentalis* 'Little Gem'

Thuja occidentalis 'Pyramidalis'   Zone 2
(Pyramidal Arborvitae)

668   A beautiful accent plant. Slow growing, very slender, compact
plant with soft dark-green fan shaped foliage. A large plant in Southern
latitudes is nine to ten feet tall; however, it grows taller in the Northwest
as a perfect pyramid without trimming. Sun or shade.
                                    Planting Group 1

Thuja occidentalis 'Woodwardi'   Zone 2
669   Widely grown dense globular Thuja with rich green foliage.
Usually a nice tree to five feet, but with age can get too large. Maintains
its shape without pruning.   Planting Group 1

Thuja orientalis 'Aurea Nana'   Zone 6
(Berckman's Arborvitae or Dwarf Golden Arborvitae)

670   Most popular dwarf arborvitae, seldom more than four feet.
Slow growing, dense pointed globe with golden-yellow branches year
around. Hardy to heat, cold and dry conditions, and best kept out
of range of dogs.   Planting Group 1

669   *Thuja occidentalis* 'Woodwardi'

671 Thuja orientalis 'Beverleyensis'

672 Tsuga canadensis

Thuja orientalis 'Beverleyensis'   Zone 5
(Beverley Hills Arborvitae)

671 Bright golden foliage on this narrow specimen. At twelve feet
is usually four to five feet wide. Requires full sun to maintain its
golden color.   Planting Group 1

Tsuga canadensis   Zone 3
(Canadian Hemlock)

672 Grows to a large pyramidal tree with horizontal branches which
have pendulous tips. Widely grown as a dense hedge in the Northwest.
For this type, prune when young.   Planting Group 1

Tsuga canadensis 'Sargentii'   Zone 4
(Weeping Sargent Hemlock)

673 A weeping form of the Canadian Hemlock. Grows broader than
it does high, forming a rounded dome with the pendulous branches
reaching to the ground or over a wall.   Planting Group 1

673 Tsuga canadensis 'Sargentii'

CROSS INDEX

COMMON	BOTANICAL
Aaron's Beard	*Hypericum calycinum*
African Boxwood	*Myrsine africana*
Alberta Spruce	*Picea glauca* 'Conica'
Aleppo Pine	*Pinus halepensis*
Alpine Fir	*Abies lasiocarpa*
Angel's Trumpet	*Datura suaveolens*
Angel Wing Jasmine	*Jasminum magnificum*
Arborvitae	*Thuja*
Arizona Ash	*Fraxinus velutina*
Arizona Cypress	*Cupressus glabra*
Atlas Cedar	*Cedrus atlantica*
Australian Blue Bell	*Sollya heterophylla*
Australian Brake Fern	*Pteris tremula*
Australian Fuchsia	*Correa pulchella*
Australian Tea Tree	*Leptospernum laevigatum*
Australian Tree Fern	*Alsophila australis*
Austrian Black Pine	*Pinus nigra*
Baby's Breath	*Diosma reevesii*
Bailey Acacia	*Acacia baileyana*
Balm of Gilead	*Populus candicans*
Bamboo	*Bambusa*
Banana Shrub	*Michelia fuscata*
Banana Tree	*Musa ensete*
Barberry	*Berberis*
Banksia Rose	*Rosa banksiae*
Bearberry Cotoneaster	*Cotoneaster dammeri*
Bear's Breech	*Acanthus mollis*
Beauty Bush	*Kolkwitzia*
Bird of Paradise	*Strelitzia reginae*
Bird of Paradise Shrub	*Poinciana gilliesii*
Bird of Paradise Tree	*Strelitzia nicolai*
Birdsnest Cypress	*Chamaecyparis lawsoniana nidiformis*
Blue Spanish Fir	*Abies pinsapo glauca*
Blackwood Acacia	*Acacia melanoxylon*
Blue Atlas Cedar	*Cedrus atlantica glauca*
Blue Cocos Palm	*Cocos australis*
Blue Leadwort	*Ceratostigma plumbaginoides*
Bog Andromeda	*Andromeda polifolia*
Boston Ivy	*Ampelopsis tricuspidata veitchii*
Boston Sword Fern	*Nephrolepis exaltata*
Botanical Wonder	*Fatshedera lizei*
Bottlebrush	*Callistemon*
Bottle Tree	*Sterculia diversifolia*
Box Leaf Azara	*Azara microphylla*
Boxwood	*Buxus*
Brazilian Flame Bush	*Calliandra tweedii*
Bridal Wreath	*Spiraea vanhouttei*
Bradford Pear	*Pyrus calleryana bradford*
Brisbane Box	*Tristania*
Bristlecone Pine	*Pinus aristata*
Brazilian Pepper	*Schinus terebinthifolius*

Brush Cherry	*Eugenua myrtifolia*
Buckwheat	*Eriogonum arborescens*
Bunya Bunya	*Araucaria bidwillii*
Burford Holly	*Ilex cornuta burfordii*
Bush Anenome	*Carpenteria californica*
Bush Morning Glory	*Convolvulus cneorum*
Bushy Yate	*Eucalyptus lehmannii*
Butterfly Iris	*Moraea iridioides*
California Big Tree	*Sequoia giganteum*
California Christmas Tree	*Cedrus deodara*
California Fan Palm	*Washingtonia filifera*
California Pepper Tree	*Schinus molle*
California Privet	*Ligustrum ovalifolium*
Camphor Tree	*Cinnamomum camphora*
Camphor Tree	*Camphora officinarum*
Canary Bird Bush	*Crotalaria agatiflora*
Canary Island Pine	*Pinus canariensis*
Cape Honeysuckle	*Tecoma capensis*
Cape Plumbago	*Plumbago capensis*
Carob	*Ceratonia siliqua*
Carolina Cherry	*Prunus caroliniana*
Carolina Jessamine	*Gelsemium sempervirens*
Carrot Wood	*Cupaniopsis anacardioides*
Catalina Cherry	*Prunus integrifolia lyonii*
Catalina Ironwood	*Lyonothamnus*
Cat's Claw	*Bignonia chamberlaynii*
Cedar	*Cedrus*
Cedar of Lebanon	*Cedrus libani*
Chile Jasmine	*Mandevilla suaveolens*
Chilian Guava	*Myrtus ugni*
Chinese Flame Tree	*Koelreuteria bipinnata*
Chinese Hollygrape	*Mahonia lomariifolia*
Cinquefoil	*Potentilla*
Coast Live Oak	*Quercus agrifolia*
Coast Redwood	*Sequoia sempervirens*
Colorado Spruce	*Picea pungens*
Copper Beech	*Fagus sylvatica purpurea*
Coral Bark Maple	*Acer palmatum Sangokaku*
Coral Gum	*Eucalyptus torquata*
Cork Oak	*Quercus suber*
Crape Myrtle	*Lagerstroemia*
Crimson King Maple	*Acer platanoides Crimson King*
Creeping Fig	*Ficus repens*
Cup of Gold Vine	*Solandra guttata*
Currant	*Ribes*
Cutleaf White Birch	*Betula alba laciniata*
Cycad	*Cycas*
Cypress	*Chamaecyparis or cupressocyparis or cupressus*
Date Palm	*Phoenix canariensis*
Dawn Redwood	*Metasequoia glyptostroboides*
Dwarf Natal Plum	*Carissa grandiflora prostrata*
Desert Gum	*Eucalyptus rudis*
Desert Willow Pittosporum	*Pittosporum phillyraeoides*
Diamond Leaf Pittosporum	*Pittosporum rhombifolium*
Dogwood	*Cornus*
Douglas Fir	*Pseudotsuga taxifolia*
Dracena Palm	*Cordyline indivisa*
Dusty Miller	*Centaurea cineraria*
Dwarf Balsam Fir	*Abies balsamea nana*
Dwarf Blue Gum	*Eucalyptus globulus compacta*
Easter Lily Vine	*Beaumontia grandiflora*
Egyptian Paper Reed	*Cyperus papyrus*
Elm	*Ulmus*
English Laurel	*Prunus laurocerasus*

Japanese Lace Fern	*Polystichum setosum*
Japanese Maple	*Acer palmatum*
Japanese Pittosporum	*Pittosporum tobira*
Japanese Privet	*Ligustrum japonica*
Japanese Red Pine	*Pinus densiflora*
Japanese Spurge	*Pachysandra terminalis*
Jelecote (or Mexican) Pine	*Pinus patula*
Kafir Lily	*Clivia miniata*
Kafir Plum	*Harpephyllum caffrum*
Kangaroo Ivy	*Cissus antarctica*
Kanooka Box	*Tristania laurina*
Karo Pittosporum	*Pittosporum crassifolium*
King Palm	*Seaforthia elegans*
Kinnikinnick	*Arctostaphylos uva-ursi*
Kupuka Tree	*Griselinia littoralis*
Lady Palm	*Rhapis excelsa*
Lavender	*Lavandula*
Lavender Starflower	*Grewia caffra*
Lavender Trumpet Vine	*Bignonia violacea*
Leather Leaf Fern	*Aspidium capense*
Lemon Leaf	*Gaultheria*
Lemon Verbena	*Lippia citriodora*
Lemonade Berry	*Rhus integrifolia*
Lemon Scented Gum	*Eucalyptus citriodora*
Lilac	*Syringa vulgaris*
Lilac Melaleuca	*Melaleuca decussata*
Lilac Vine	*Hardenbergia comptoniana*
Lili Pili Tree	*Eugenia smithii*
Lily of the Nile	*Agapanthus*
Lily of the Valley Shrub	*Pieris japonica*
Lily Turfs	*Liriope muscari*
Linden	*Tilia*
Locust	*Robinia (also Gleditsia)*
Lombardy Popular	*Populus nigra italica*
Loquat	*Eriobotrya*
Madagascar Jasmine	*Stephanotis floribunda*
Madrone	*Arbutus menziesii*
Maidenhair Tree	*Ginkgo*
Manzanita	*Arctostaphylos*
Matilija Poppy	*Romneya coulteri*
Mayten Tree	*Maytenus*
Mediterranean Fan Palm	*Chamaerops humilis*
Mexican Blue Palm	*Erythea armata*
Mexican Fan Palm	*Washingtonia robusta*
Mexican Orange	*Choisya ternata*
Mexican (or Jelecote) Pine	*Pinus patula*
Meyer Lemon	*Citrus*
Mimosa	*Albizia*
Mirror Plant	*Coprosma*
Mock Orange	*Philadelphus virginalis*
Modesto Ash	*Fraxinus velutina* 'Glabra'
Monterey Cypress	*Cupressus macrocarpa*
Monterey Pine	*Pinus radiata*
Moraine Locust	*Gleditsia*
Morrocco Creeper	*Convolvulus mauritanicus*
Mother Fern	*Asplenium bulbiferum*
Mountain Ash	*Sorbus*
Mountain Laurel	*Kalmia latifolia*
Mugho Pine	*Pinus mugo mughus*
Mulberry	*Morus*
Myrtle	*Myrtus*
Natal Plum	*Carissa*
Neantha Bella Palm	*Chamaedorea elegans*
Nest Spruce	*Picea excelsa nidiformis*

Salal	*Gaultheria*
Sandankwa	*Viburnum suspensum*
Scarlet Trumpet Vine	*Bignonia cherere*
Scarlet Oak	*Quercus coccinea*
Scarlet Wisteria Tree	*Daubentonia tripetii*
Schwedleri Maple	*Acer platanoides schwedleri*
Scotch Broom	*Cytisus*
Scotch Pine	*Pinus sylvestris*
Sea Urchin Tree	*Hakea laurina*
Senegal Date Palm	*Phoenix reclinata*
Senisa	*Leucophyllum frutescens*
Shademaster Locust	*Gleditsia*
Shamel Ash	*Fraxinus uhdei*
Shore Juniper	*Juniper conferta*
Shoe Button Spiraea	*Spiraea prunifolia*
Shrimp Plant	*Beloperone guttata*
Shrubby Yew	*Podocarpus maki*
Siberian Grape	*Mahonia bealei*
Silver Lace Vine	*Polygonum aubertii*
Silk Tassel Bush	*Garrya elliptica*
Silk Oak Tree	*Grevillea robusta*
Silver Berry	*Elaeagnus*
Silver Dollar Eucalyptus	*Eucalyptus polyanthemos*
Silver Leaf Cotoneaster	*Cotoneaster pannosa*
Silver Maple	*Acer saccharinum*
Silver Mountain Gum	*Eucalyptus pulverulenta*
Silver Tree	*Leucadendron*
Single Mother Fern	*Polystichum angulare*
Smoke Tree	*Cotinus coggygria, Rhus cotinus*
Snail Seed	*Cocculus*
Snowball	*Viburnum opulus sterile*
Sourwood Sorrel Tree	*Oxydendrum arboreum*
Southern Magnolia	*Magnolia grandiflora*
Spanish Bayonet	*Yucca aloifolia*
Spanish Broom	*Spartium junceum*
Spanish Dagger	*Yucca gloriosa*
Staghorn Fern	*Platycerium*
Star Acacia	*Acacia verticillata*
Star Jasmine	*Rhynchospermum jasminoides*
Star Pine	*Araucaria excelsa*
St. John's Bread	*Ceratonia siliqua*
St. Johnswort	*Hypericum patulum henryi*
Strawberry Tree	*Arbutus unedo*
Sugar Bush	*Rhus ovata*
Sugar Plum Tree	*Lagunaria pattersoni*
Sumac	*Rhus typhina*
Sunburst Locust	*Gleditsia*
Swamp Tea Tree	*Melaleuca leucadendra*
Sweet Broom	*Genista racemosa*
Sweetgum	*Liquidambar*
Sweet Olive	*Osmanthus fragrans*
Sweet Pea Shrub	*Polygala dalmaisiana*
Sweetshade	*Hymenosporum flavum*
Sweetspire	*Itea*
Sweet Viburnum	*Viburnum odoratissimum*
Sycamore	*Platanus*
Table Mountain Pine	*Pinus densiflora* 'Umbraculifera'
Tamarisk	*Tamarix tetrandra*
Tanyosho Pine	*Pinus densiflora* 'Umbraculifera'
Tarata Pittosporum	*Pittosporum eugenioides*
Tasmanian Tree Fern	*Dicksonia antarctica*
Tawhiwhi Pittosporum	*Pittosporum tenuifolium (P. nigricans)*
Tea Tree	*Leptospermum*
Tecomaria	*Tecoma*

PLANTS WITH WHITE FLOWERS

Abelia	Escallonia	Nerium
Azalea	Eugenia	Osmanthus
Acanthus	Gardenia	Philadelphus
Aesculus	Gleditsia	Photinia
Althaea	Hebe	Pieris
Bouvardia	Hibiscus	Pittosporum
Camellia	Hydrangea	Polygonum
Calluna	Jasminum	Prunus
Carissa	Lantana	Pyracantha
Carpenteria	Leptospermum	Raphiolepis
Catalpa	Leucothoe	Rhododendron
Choisya	Ligustrum	Rhynchospermum
Cistus	Loropetalum	Romneya
Clematis	Lyonothamnus	Solanum
Convolvulus	Magnolia	Sparmannis
Cornus	Malus	Spiraea
Cortaderia	Marguerite	Stephanotis
Crataegus	Melaleuca	Syringa
Cytissus	Moraea	Viburnum
Datura	Murraya	Wister
Deutzia	Myrtus	Yuc
Diosma	Nandina	

PLANTS WITH YELLOW TO ORANGE FLOWERS

Abutilon	Euryops	Koelreuteria
Acacia	Fremontia	Lonicera
Azalea	Gelsemium	Mahonia
Berberis	Genista	Marguerite
Bignonia	Grevillea	Poinciana
Bougainvillea	Hibbertia	Rhododendron
Cassia	Hibiscus	Solandra
Clivia	Hymenosporum	Spartium
Corokia	Hypericum	Strelitzia
Crotalaria	Jasmine	Streptosolen
Cytisus	Kerria	Thunbergia
Daubentonia		

PLANTS WITH RED OR PINK FLOWERS

Abelia
Abutilon
Albizia
Aesculus
Azalea
Bignonia
Bougainvillea
Calliandra
Callistemon
Calluna
Camellia
Campsis
Ceris
Chorisia
Clematis
Cornus
Crataegus

Correa
Cyponia
Daphne
Diosma
Erica
Escallonia
Eucalyptus
Fuchsia
Hibiscus
Hydrangea
Kalmia
Kolkwitzia
Lagerstroemia
Lagunaria
Lantana
Leptospernum
Magnolia

Malus
Mandevilla
Melianthus
Melaleuca
Metrosideros
Nerium
Passiflora
Prunus
Punica
Raphiolepis
Rhododendron
Ribes
Stenocarpus
Tamarix
Tecoma
Weigela
Wisteria

PLANTS WITH BLUE OR VIOLET FLOWERS

Azalea
Bauhinia
Bignonia
Bougainvillea
Brunfelsia
Ceanothus
Ceratostigma
Clematis
Echium
Fuchsia
Grewia

Hardenbergia
Hebe
Jacaranda
Lantana
Lavandula
Leucophyllum
Liriope
Melia
Paulownia
Pleroma
Plumbago

Polygala
Rosmarinus
Solanum
Sollya
Syringa
Teucrium
Veronica
Wisteria

FRAGRANT TREES AND SHRUBS

Acacia	*Eucalyptus*	*Myrtus*
Baccharis	*Gardenia*	*Osmanthus*
Bouvardia	*Hymenosporum*	*Philadelphus*
Brunfelsia	*Jasmine*	*Pittosporum*
Camphor	*Laurus*	*Rhododendrons*
Carissa	*Lavandula*	*Robinia*
Cestrum	*Ligustrum*	*Rhynchospermum*
Choisya	*Libocedrus*	*Rosmarinus*
Citrus	*Lippia*	*Sarcococca*
Clematis	*Lonicera*	*Spartium*
Cypress	*Magnolia*	*Stephanotis*
Daphne	*Mandevilla*	*Syringa*
Datura	*Michelia*	*Viburnum*
Diosma	*Murraya*	*Wisteria*

SEASHORE PLANTS

Abelia	*Euryops*	*Metrosideros*
Acacia	*Fraxinus*	*Myoporum*
Barberry	*Garrya*	*Myrica*
Camphor	*Gaultheria*	*Pittosporum*
Ceratonia	*Gelsemium*	*Plumbago*
Ceratostigma	*Griselinia*	*Raphiolepis*
Cistus	*Hakea*	*Rhus ovata*
Coprosma	*Hebe*	*Rosmarinus*
Correa	*Hypericum*	*Schinus*
Corynocarpus	*Juniper*	*Solandra*
Cupaniopsis	*Lantana*	*Spartium*
Cupressus	*Leptospermum*	*Tecoma*
Dracaena	*Leucophyllum*	*Ulmus*
Duranta	*Liquidambar*	*Viburnum*
Echium	*Lonicera*	*Veronica*
Escallonia	*Marguerites*	
Eugenia	*Melaleuca*	

TREES AND SHRUBS FOR DRY PLACES

Abelia
Acacia
Albizia
Arbutus
Arctostaphylos
Atriplex
Baccharis
Berberis
Buddleia
Buxus
Callistemon
Cassia
Ceanothus
Ceratonia
Cercis
Chamaelaucium
Cistus
Cordyline
Cortaderia
Cotoneaster

Cotinus
Cupressus
Cytisus
Dodonaea
Echium
Elaeagnus
Eriogonum
Eucalyptus
Feijoa
Fremontia
Garrya
Grevillea
Hakea
Hypericum
Juniper
Lagerstroemia
Lantana
Lavandula
Leptospermum
Mahonia

Melaleuca
Myoporum
Nerium
Olea
Pinus
Phormium
Pittosporum
Prunus
Pyracantha
Quercus
Rhamnus
Rhus
Robinia
Rosmarinus
Schinus
Senecio
Sorbus
Xylosma
Yucca

TREES AND SHRUBS FOR DAMP PLACES

Abutilon
Acer
Alnus
Aucuba
Bamboo
Betula
Clivia
Coprosma

Cornus
Cyperus
Equisetum
Fraxinus
Fuchsia
Kalmia
Leucothoe
Ligustrum

Lonicera
Metasequoia
Salix
Skimmia
Solandra
Sequoia
Spiraea

DEER-RESISTANT PLANTS FOR ORNAMENTAL USE*

Abies spp
Abutilon spp
Acacia spp
Acer negundo
Acer palmatum
Agapanthus africanus
Agave spp
Ajuga spp
Albizia spp
Aloe spp
Araucaria spp
Arbutus unedo
Beaucarnea recurvata
Berberis spp
Brachychiton populneum
Buddleia davidii
Buxus spp
Cactaceae spp
Calliandra tweedii
Calycanthus occidentalis
Carpenteria californica
Cassia spp
Casuarina stricta
Cedrus spp
Ceratonia siliqua
Cercis occidentalis
Chamaecyparis spp
Chamaerops humilis
Choisya ternata
Chrysanthemum frutescens
Chrysanthemum maximum
Cistus spp
Clematis spp
Coprosma repens
Cordyline australis
Cornus capitata
Correa spp
Cotinus coggygria
Cotoneaster spp
Crataegus spp
Cupressus spp

Cycas spp
Cytisus scoparius
Daphne spp
Datura spp
Delphinium spp
Diosma ericoides
Diosma pulchrum
Diospyros
Dodonaea viscosa
Echium fastuosum
Erythea armata
Erythea edulis
Escallonia spp
Eucalyptus spp
Ficus spp
Forsythia
Fraxinus velutina
Fraxinus velutina glabra
Gaultheria shallon
Gelsemium sempervirens
Genista monosperma
Ginkgo biloba
Hakea suaveolens
Hedera
Helleborus spp
Ilex spp
Iris spp
Jasminum spp
Juniperus spp
Kerria japonica
Kniphofia uvaria
Lantana
Lavandula spp
Leptospermum spp
Lyonothamnus floribundus
Magnolia spp
Mahonia spp
Maytenus boaria
Melaleuca leucadendra
Melianthus major
Mesembryanthemum spp

Metrosideros tomentosa
Myoporum laetum
Myrica californica
Myrtus communis
Nandina domestica
Nerium oleander
Olea europaea
Osteospermum fruticosum
Paeonia suffruticosa
Parkinsonia aculeata
Penstemon spp
Phoenix spp
Phormium tenax
Picea spp
Pinus spp
Pittosporum spp
Platanus racemosa
Potentilla fruticosa
Prunus caroliniana
Rhododendron spp.
    (except azalea-leaved varieties)
Rhus ovata
Robinia pseudoacacia
Romneya coulteri
Rosmarinus officinalis
Sambucus
Scabiosa spp
Schinus
Solanum spp
Spartium junceum
Syringa vulgaris
Syzygium paniculatum
Taxus spp
Tecomaria capensis
Teucrium fruticans
Thuja spp
Trachycarpus fortunei
Tradescantia spp
Vinca spp
Washingtonia spp
Yucca spp

*Some of the plants will be resistant in some areas and not in others.

PLANTS RESISTANT
TO ARMILLARIA ROOT ROT (OAK ROOT FUNGUS)

ORNAMENTALS
PLANTS IMMUNE OR HIGHLY RESISTANT

Botanical Name	Common Name	Botanical Name	Common Name
Abies concolor	Colorado or White Fir	Brachychiton populneum	Kurrajong Bottle Tree
Acacia decurrens var. mollis	Black Wattle	Buxus sempervirens	Common Box
Acacia latifolia	.... Acacia	Ilex aquifolium	English Holly
Acacia verticillata	Star Acacia	Lonicera nitida	Bush or Box Honeysuckle
Acer macrophyllum	Big-Leaf Maple	Pinus canariensis	Canary Pine
Arbutus menziesii	Madrone	Pinus torreyana	Torrey Pine
Berberis aquifolium	Oregon Grape	Prunus ilicifoli	Holly-leaved Cherry
Berberis nevinii	Nevin Mahonia	Prunus lyonii ...	Catalina Cherry

PLANTS MODERATELY RESISTANT

Abelia grandiflora	Glossy Abelia	Ligustrum japonicum	Japanese Privet
Acer negundo var. californicum	California Box Elder	Malus prunifolia	Pear-leaf Crabapple
Berberis darwinii	Darwin Barberry	Myrtus communis	True Myrtle
Berberis thunbergii	Japanese Barberry	Pittosporum tobira	Japanese Pittosporum
Berberis wilsoniae	Wilson Barberry	Prunus sp	Black Damas Plum
Chamaecyparis lawsoniana	Lawson Cypress	Prunus avium	Mazzard Sweet Cherry
Cydonia oblonga	Quince	Prunus Salicina	Satsuma Plum
Elaeagnus commutata	Silverberry	Prunus Mexicana	Big Tree Plum
Euonymus japonica	Evergreen Burning Bush	Prunus Mume	Japanese Apricot
Grevillea robusta	Silk Oak	Pseudotsuga menziesli	Douglas Fir
Hebe andersonii	Anderson Speedwell	Pyracantha coccinea	Scarlet Firethorn
Hebe speciosa	Showy or Imperial Speedwell	Pyracantha lalandii	Laland Firethorn
		Spiraea prunifolia	Bridal Wreath Spirea

RESISTANT

Abutilon spp	Abutilon or Flowering-Maple	Liriodendron tulipifera	Tulip Tree
Arctostaphylos spp	Manzanita	Morus spp	Mulberry
Catalpa spp	Catalpa	Nerium oleander	Oleander
Ceanothus spp	Ceanothus	Philadelphus spp	Mock-Orange
Cinnamon camphora	Camphor Tree	Pittosporum spp	Pittosporum
Cistus spp	Rock Rose	Platanus spp	Plane Tree or Sycamore
Eugenia spp	Eugenia	Rhaphiolepis spp	Rhaphiolepis
Eucalyptus spp	Eucalyptus	Rhus spp	Sumac
Fraxinus spp	Ash	Robinia spp	Locust
Hebe spp	Hebe	Tamarix aphylla	Tamarisk, Athel
Hedera helix	Ivy	Tibouchina semidecandra	
Hibiscus spp	Rose Mallow and Hibiscus		Pleroma, Glorybush or Princess Flower
Lagerstroemia indica	Crape-Myrtle	Ulmus spp	Elm
Liquidambar stryaciflua	Sweet Gum	Various genera	Palms

FRUITS AND NUTS
IMMUNE OR HIGHLY RESISTANT

Carya illinoensis	Pecan	Juglans hindsii	California Black Walnut
Castanea dentata	American Chestnut	Malus loensis	Prairie Crabapple
Castanea sativa	European Chestnut	Malus sp	French Crabapple
Diospyros kaki	Japanese Persimmon	Persea americana	Mexican Avocado
Diospyros virginiana	Common Persimmon	Prunus americana	American Plum
Ficus carica cv. kadota	Kadota Fig	Prunus cerasifera	Myrobalan Plum
Fiscus carica cv. mission	Mission Fig	Pyrus communis	French Pear

AFTERWORD

In the Introduction of this book I told you of the aims I had in mind when I wrote it.

Now, in Conclusion — let me add that it is time to stop talking to your plants all the time and *listen* (with your eyes) for a change. They will tell you of their aches and pains — yellow, droopy, brown-edged leaves and/or bent-over, stringy branches and plants reaching for the light — and, in many other ways.

I hope you enjoy this work,

Gordon Courtright